TRULY YOURS

ONE HUNDRED AND FIFTY YEARS

OF

PLAY PUBLISHING

&

SERVICE TO THE THEATRE

SAMUEL FRENCH Ltd
LONDON

SAMUEL FRENCH Inc
New York

Samuel French Ltd
26 Southampton Street
London WC2E 7JE

Samuel French (Australia) Pty Ltd
Dominie Pty Ltd 8 Cross Street
Brookvale NSW 2100

Samuel French Inc
25 West 45th Street
New York 10036

Samuel French Inc
7623 Sunset Boulevard
Hollywood

Samuel French (Canada) Ltd
80 Richmond Street East
Toronto Ontario M5C 1P1

ISBN 0 573 00150 2

Preface

As we move into the last half of our second century we may surely be forgiven if our corporate mind takes an autobiographical turn and indulges in a few historical jottings. To call these a History of French's would be presumptuous. There may be material here for a history, and one day it may be compiled—perhaps by a computer with full retrieval facilities for students of Theatre History—but meantime let us reminisce gently, with no great sense of self-importance, and of course no false modesty.

If Voltaire were alive today he might be tempted to say "Si French's n'existait pas, il faudrait l'enventer". Which is but another way of saying that we fill a long-felt want. Over the years as the need has changed so French's has changed to meet it. Every age has its bogey-man. For us in the 1950s, our bogey was TV. Would it be the death of the Amateur Theatre, with everyone staying at home and becoming a nation of watchers rather than doers? Well we now know it wasn't the end, though in the short term it may have looked as though it would have that effect. In the longer term it may have contributed to an increasing awareness of the performing arts, and to the rising standards among amateurs. We would hesitate to be dogmatic about the effects, but today the demand for technical books on the theatre is greater than it has ever been, and our background and experience of the theatre have provided the foundation for The Theatre Bookshop.

In the 1970s our bogey has been the increasing complexity of taxation. The staff of dedicated pen-pushers who once carried in their heads every intricacy of every author's account could not in the nature of things be expected to be with us still, nor could they cope today if they were. We knew when they retired they would be irreplaceable. Today we employ our second generation computer to do their work. A blessing in speed; but once upon a time you could walk into the Royalty Accounts office, open a ledger for yourself and read the whole financial history of a play. Today, alas, you can only talk to the computer by appointment, and it is advisable to have an interpreter standing by.

What we are offering in these pages is by way of being an appetizer. The main course may follow one day, but not yet. Our history is spread around the world wherever English is spoken, and because we are still making it we find it hard to assess the more recent past. For this reason our reminiscences cease about fifteen years ago. Everything is important to us, nothing is trivial; what would be interesting and what dull will have to be decided in time by someone who is not involved in preparing the feast.

Meanwhile, we must express our grateful thanks to all those who have jogged our mind and helped with contributions of historical information. In particular the Theatre Museum, and Roger Stoddard of the Houghton Library, Harvard.

NW

M Abbott Van Nostrand

Chairman of Samuel French Inc 1952— & Samuel French Ltd 1975—

Beginnings

ONE HUNDRED AND FIFTY years is a goodly age. For us it covers six whole reigns and a long way into a seventh. London was very different when this story begins in 1830. It was the year in which George IV died and his younger brother William became King. Victoria, his niece, during whose life the business of French's was to develop into a theatrical institution, was only eleven. Travel was still by stage coach at the spanking pace of ten miles an hour, although Stephenson's Rocket had just been completed, and the Liverpool and Manchester Railroad formally opened. The Iron Duke was Prime Minister; Charles Dickens was a short-hand writer in Doctors' Commons; and *Black Eyed Susan* had just made theatrical history by running for 150 performances at the Surrey Theatre. Across the Atlantic General Jackson was the seventh President of the United States, and the population of New York was just edging 203,000. Thomas Hailes Lacy was a young man of twenty: Samuel French was only nine.

Samuel French's ancestry is well recorded at least as far back as the first quarter of the seventeenth century. Thomas French, who was born in England about 1612, left for America in 1646, and after a brief stay in Dorchester, Massachusetts, settled in Braintree. His seven children, all born in America, were given names that were either biblical or reflected the more highly considered virtues of the times such as "Temperance" and "Dependence": "Experience" and "Silence" also occurred among the women's names in the family.

Our Samuel, the third of that name in six generations, was born in Randolph, Massachusetts, in 1821. Nothing is known about his early life, but in the late 1830s, at a time when there was a major depression in New York, he was selling literature cheaply produced as Mammoth Weeklies (the equivalent of our modern paperbacks). He evidently had some entrepreneurial flair, and was involved in various ventures, including selling shoes, before trying his hand at play publishing in the 1850s. For several years before this, he had acted as an agent for William Taylor & Co of New York, then the publishers of the principal contemporary American collections of British and American drama, and in 1854 he began to publish his own *French's American Drama*. His next move was to buy the plates from which Taylor's plays were printed, so beginning his slow but sure rise to the peak of American play publishing. He bought up every set of printing plates that he could lay his hands on, thus absorbing his competitors. There was probably very little if any selection made, or judgement of the worth of the individual material, but he soon built himself a virtual monopoly, incorporating nearly all his purchases and much of *French's American Drama* into two new series, *French's Standard Drama* and *French's Minor Drama*. It was not long before French had the most extensive and widely distributed catalogue in the USA—as early as 1856 he was advertising 100,000 plays on hand.* The majority of these plays were reprints, but French did publish first editions of several American plays important to the professional theatre—plays such as *Uncle Tom's Cabin* by George L Aiken and *The Poor of New York* by Dion Boucicault. These plays were released for publication by their authors as a result of the passing of the 1856 Copyright Law, which granted American playwrights the "sole right . . . to act perform or represent their works", but it was not until many years later that French was able to claim performance royalties for his authors.

Although the Samuel French enterprise catered for both the professional and amateur theatre, it was French's role in encouraging amateur dramatics that allowed him to dominate American play publishing. From his premises in Nassau Street, New York, he supplied everything the budding amateur dramatic group might need—make-up, wigs, costumes, lights and even sets, as well as the plays themselves—everything, in fact, apart from acting ability, and he even tried to supply that in the form of how-to-act books!

* All Samuel French's figures should be taken guardedly. Later Wentworth Hogg was probably also guilty of adding the occasional zero for affect. French was not always reliable in dates either.

In 1870, French brought his only son Thomas Henry into the firm, which became Samuel French & Son shortly afterwards. Thomas was soon left in charge of the New York office, for his father moved to England in 1872, having bought out the somewhat older business of Thomas Hailes Lacy in London.

How French and Lacy came together in the first place is not known, but they acted as each other's agent across the Atlantic, both being in the play publishing business.

We know rather more about Lacy's pre-publishing days than those of French. He was born in 1809, and spent the early years of his theatrical career as a provincial actor, allegedly of some repute. He had been born Thomas Lacy Hailes, but for some reason—professional vanity, perhaps?—he reversed the last two names. His first recorded appearance in London was in 1828 at the Olympic Theatre, as Lenoir in *The Foundling of the Forest*, a play which he was later to publish. After acting as stage manager at the Windsor Theatre, he progressed to the general management of the theatre, and in 1841 he became manager of the Theatre Royal, Sheffield. Around this time he met his future wife, Frances Dalton Cooper, known professionally as Miss Fanny Cooper, an actress who was "one of the most talented, lovely and virtuous beings in the world" if a contemporary biographer is to be believed. The wedding took place on the 25th January 1842 at St Paul's Church, London, just around the corner from our present premises in Southampton Street.

After their marriage the couple continued to tour the provinces, with Mrs Lacy making frequent appearances at the Theatre Royal, Covent Garden, and Lacy managing to combine his acting with the general and stage management of various theatres. He also found the time to write several plays.

In 1844, the Lacys were engaged at the Sadler's Wells Theatre, London, by Mrs Warner and Mr Phelps to support their "legitimate campaign" to make Sadler's Wells "what a theatre ought to be—a place for justly representing the works of our great dramatic poets . . . where all can see and hear at a price fairly within the habitual means of all". These noble sentiments did not prevent Lacy from quitting his engagement some three months later, followed shortly by his wife. At the end of this year, Mr and Mrs Lacy went on another successful starring tour of the provinces, returning to Sadler's Wells in time for the second season under Mrs Warner and Mr Phelps. Shortly after this Lacy withdrew from the stage to devote himself full-time to play publishing, an area in which he had been building an interest during his years in the theatre.

FRENCH'S
AMERICAN DRAMA.

No. 1.

Grosvenor

A

Mid Summer-Night's Dream.

A COMEDY, IN THREE ACTS.

BY

WILLIAM SHAKSPEARE.

With Cost of Characters, Stage Business, Costumes, Relative Positions. etc. etc.

Mendelssohn's Music of this Play may be had of T. GOODWIN, No. 7 Vandam-st. New-York.

NEW-YORK:
SAMUEL FRENCH,
121 NASSAU-STREET.

PRICE,   12½ CENTS.

The first play published under Samuel French's Imprint

Bibliotheca Histrionica.—Part the Second

CATALOGUE

OF

DRAMATIC LITERATURE;

COMPRISING

ANCIENT & MODERN PLAYS;

SHAKESPERIANA;

THEATRICAL BIOGRAPHY AND CRITICISM;

CONTROVERSIAL WORKS FOR AND AGAINST THE STAGE;

HISTORY OF THEATRES,

LONDON, IRISH, SCOTTISH, AND PROVINCIAL—THEIR ARCHITECTURE AND TOPOGRAPHY;

PLAY-BILLS IN GREAT VARIETY;

PORTRAITS, AUTOGRAPHS, COSTUMES, & MUSIC;

NOW ON SALE BY

T. H. LACY,

THEATRICAL BOOKSELLER,

17, Wellington-street, Strand,

LONDON.

FOR READY MONEY ONLY.

CATALOGUES, PRICE 3d. (RETURNED TO PURCHASERS.)

ORDERS BY POST, ENCLOSING A REMITTANCE, EXECUTED BY RETURN; ABOVE 10s., CARRIAGE FREE.

Books Bought on Commission.

BOOKBINDING IN THE BEST STYLE, ON THE LOWEST TERMS.

The Title Page of Lacy's Catalogue (Part II) [1854]

In February 1830, the English Opera House had been destroyed by fire, and the opportunity had been taken to extend Wellington Street as far as the Strand while building a new theatre—the Lyceum—and it was here that Lacy commenced his business—at No. 11. Later the street numbers were changed, and his shop became No. 17. With a "quick appreciation of the requirements of the histrionic profession", Lacy soon expanded his trade in "dramatic works, ancient and modern", developing a publishing business which had been less extensively carried on some years before by various publisher-booksellers (we know of Miller, Kenneth and Harris) around the Covent Garden area. The extensive and intimate knowledge of theatrical literature which Lacy had acquired during his years in the theatre proved to be of great service in the early days of the business, which expanded rapidly as Lacy acquired more and more titles. He did this by buying up the plates of earlier publishers, as Samuel French was to do in America; Dunscombe, Webster, Oxberry and Cumberland all came into his grasp. The works of John Cumberland were the most extensive, and Lacy became the proprietor of *Cumberland's British Theatre* (*printed from acting copies as performed at the Theatres Royal, London*) and *Cumberland's Minor Theatre*. Lacy also published his own acting editions of plays and by 1873 *Lacy's Acting Edition of Plays* ran to 99 volumes and contained 1,485 pieces. One of his early catalogues lists such intriguing play titles as *I've Eaten My Friend*, *Tooth-ache* and *Wanted, 1000 Milliners*.

Apart from plays, Lacy's little shop in Wellington Street was well-stocked with "Shakesperiana; Theatrical Biography and Criticism; Controversial works for and against the Stage; Play bills in Great Variety; Portraits, Autographs, Costumes and Music", all available "for ready money only". As his trade increased, he was eventually forced to find larger premises, and in 1859, the business moved to 89 The Strand, where it was to remain for the next forty-odd years. Lacy himself continued for only the next fourteen years until the Spring of 1872, when he transferred the business and stock to Samuel French. His retirement was rather short-lived, however, as he died on 1st August the following year.

The "valuable theatrical and miscellaneous library" which he had amassed over the years and "an extensive and valuable collection of portraits . . . comprising theatrical performers, dramatists, composers and others connected with the stage, including several in the finest state and of great rarity" were sold by auction on 24th November and 1st December respectively by Messrs Sotheby, Wilkinson and Hodge, auctioneers of literary property and works of illustrative art, at their house No. 13 Wellington Street,

Strand WC. The sales, made in accordance with Lacy's will, were obviously important ones, and the latter collection which required two days must have been extensive. With the exception of a few legacies (including £100 to the Battersea Dogs' Home) and two small annuities, Lacy bequeathed his property to the Royal General Theatrical Fund, of which he had been a director, to be preserved as "The Lacy Bequest".

Samuel French paid his first visit to this country in 1859, five years after starting up his business in New York. Whether he first met Lacy then, or had known him before, is not clear; but certainly about this time the two of them were doing business together, and continued to do so over the next decade or so. French, we are told, had suffered for years from asthma, and came over here again in 1872 deciding to make his home in London. He was reputedly influenced by the impenetrable London fogs which were kinder to his respiratory condition than the bracing winters and stifling summers of New York. Lacy, in his early sixties, with no immediate family who were interested in carrying on the business, no doubt felt it was time to retire and so he sold out to French.

Under a contract dated 19th March 1872, French acquired the business for £5,000. £3,000 was paid immediately, with four promissory notes for £500 each to be paid on the 1st July in each succeeding year. "French, late Lacy" was now the legend that greeted passers-by in The Strand, and business under Mr French carried on much the same as it had done under Mr Lacy.

On his arrival in England, French had bought a house in Addison Road, Holland Park. It was a purchase that was destined to have a profound effect on the business. The house, No. 32, belonged to one Joseph Hogg, a master tailor. Opposite lived the Mansells, a family with a considerable interest in the Arts, who held occasional musical and theatrical evenings. They were friendly with the Hoggs, and it may have been at one of these soirées that French met Joseph Hogg. In any event, two years later Joseph's son Wentworth left his job in the wine-trade and went to work for French as his Manager. Wentworth Hogg's value to French must have been far beyond his salary—whatever that may have been. In the next twenty years he had compiled—written would have been a better word—the first *Guide to Selecting Plays*, a catalogue that described in considerable detail every play that the firm controlled, and that occupied two years of his spare time. The book, which sold for a shilling, received a rapturous press, and was also well-received by amateur theatre groups. A contemporary edition of the *Hairdressers' Chronicle and Trade Journal* gives the best insight into the conduct of amateur theatricals of the time: "... *a dramatic entertainment is among the most cheerful and pleasant ways of providing an evening's entertainment ... it delights the elder and gratifies the younger members of the family circle; while on a more extended scale amateur theatricals are provocative of merriment, especially when laughable pieces are represented on the temporary stage ... even the mishaps which sometimes occur in serious parts, though they may spoil the scene, are nevertheless regarded with kindly consideration.*" It is when we read in another review "*If actresses are considered unattainable or unadvisable, there are some fifty comic dramas ... in which female characters are dispensed with altogether*" that we realize the dangers and disappointments that beset the amateur Thespian in the 1880s.

Twenty-five years before Wentworth Hogg's *Guide* came out Lacy had published *The Amateur's Handbook and Guide to Home and Drawing Room Theatricals. How to get them up and how to act in them. By W J Sorrell. To which is added How to "get up" theatricals in a country house, By Captain Sock Buskin. And a supplement containing a list of suitable plays, with the number of male and female characters. Complete lists of the modern plays. The law for amateurs. The free drama. Addresses of theatrical tradesmen. And many particulars of great utility and interest.* This comprehensive booklet, no doubt brought up to date, was still on sale in the 1920s. An American edition had been published by Samuel French across the Atlantic in 1866.

Lacy's successful business continued to prosper under Samuel French and his young Manager, and some years later the London Correspondent of the *New York Times* interviewed the entrepreneur. It is a splendid interview and brings French himself gloriously to life as a person, and is in addition a highly entertaining piece of journalism—almost a parody of itself. It is quoted extensively opposite.

6

HOW FOREIGN PLAYS FIND A MARKET

THE BUSINESS OF PUBLISHING DRAMAS AND OF DISPOSING OF UNPUBLISHED ONES AN AGENCY FOR AUTHORS AND MANAGERS—HOW VARIOUS INTERESTS ARE PROTECTED—PROFITS OF PLAYWRIGHTS FROM AMERICAN THEATRES

from our own correspondent

LONDON, Thursday, Sept 19, 1878

The great thoroughfare, The Strand, is full of business houses of all descriptions. There is hardly a trade unrepresented there. The stores are equally varied in their style and appearance. Ostentation stands side by side with unpretentiousness. There are plate-glass fronts and plain shop windows, stores with brand new businesses and others that jog on under the shadow of old-fashioned predecessors. Among the latter may be classed No. 89, once the theatrical publishing-house of Mr Lacy, now the bureau of Mr Samuel French, who is the head of a similar house in New York, and where artistic and commercial wires are multifarious, and connected with many lands. Three hundred years old, it is an interesting shop, this house of theatrical publishing, and promises to become an institution of growing importance. Hardly an hour in the day that you will not see some dramatic author or manager of note going in or coming out, while distinguished amateurs and budding professionals are always to be found hunting among Mr French's world-famous library of acting editions of plays. No. 89 Strand is as well-known among theatrical people as Threadneedle Street is to a stock-broker. I had no difficulty, therefore, in fulfilling my instructions to go there and discuss the question of dramatic copyright and agency with Mr French, and I trust the result will throw a useful light upon the working of a business of so much importance to dramatic authors and theatrical managers.

"Come," said a not unpleasant voice in response to my knock. I had passed through the shop, up a narrow staircase, along a passage packed with sheets of plays fresh from the printers. I entered a plainly-furnished room, with two windows overlooking the Strand. A middle-aged gentleman was sitting at a desk busily engaged with his morning letters. He looked up at me inquiringly through a pair of spectacles. It was Mr French.

"I have called," I said, "at the request of the NEW YORK TIMES, to make some inquiries in regard to the present condition of dramatic copyright as it affects English and foreign authors, and also to ask you some questions relating to the operations of your dramatic agency."

"Yes sir," said Mr French. "I am very happy to see you, and shall be only too pleased to answer any questions you wish to ask me. Things have been said in New York which—"

"Pardon me," I said, interrupting him, "I have nothing to do with what has been said; my object is simply to give THE TIMES an idea of the present state of dramatic copyright as worked through your agency, and, if you have no objection, a sketch of the business."

"Very good, I have nothing to conceal. My business is simple and straight, and I will be glad to have you investigate the questions you ask me as fully as you wish."

"First then, Mr French," I said, "I know something of the history of theatrical publishing. Will you correct me, if I am wrong, while I recapitulate what I believe to be the history of this house? Acting editions of plays were first published for sale in the early part of this century, notably by one Dunscombe, and afterward by Cumberland, Fairbrother, Strange and others. Among the latter was Mr Lacy. . . . He bought up all other acting editions and, establishing this business, bequeathed at his death $70,000 to the Dramatic Fund, thus giving back to the profession the money he had made by it. Shortly before Lacy's death you bought his business. Is that correct?"

"Yes; Lacy found that in a business of this kind there is not room for several persons, so he bought out the rest."

"In Lacy's day, what were the conditions of dramatic copyright as between France and England?"

"Chaos . . . there was no convention of any kind then between France and England, and English translators and adapters used to take plays from the French and disguise the source whence they got them."

"But in 1852," said Mr French, "an English act of Parliament was passed. Here it is; look at it."

He handed me the copy of an act to enable her Majesty to carry out a convention with France on the subject of copyright in regard to books, plays and engravings. It gave to foreign authors a five-years right to prevent unauthorized translations of their books being published, and this was applied to plays. But the following stipulation was sufficient to endow so-called British dramatic authors with fame and fortune:

"Nothing herein contained shall be so construed as to prevent fair imitations or adaptations to the English stage of any dramatic piece or musical composition published in any foreign country."

I read no further. This was sufficient to cover the multitude of English pirates, who, in many cases, not only took the French ideas, but did so without acknowledgement even in the programmes of the play.

"Thank you, I have mastered that document. . . . What is the state of things now? . . . Will you kindly tell me what rights French authors have, how they are brought here, and how they are sold also to America French authors have, how they are bought here, and how they are sold also to America?"

"Certainly. A French author writes a play. It is produced; he is applied to by a London manager or actor—"

"Or speculator," I suggested. "Yourself, for instance."

"Yes. They make a bargain; they come to terms—an English act of Parliament of about two years ago protecting the French author and giving him proprietary rights in his plays in England."

"Then there is really an international copyright between France and England as complete as that?" I asked.

"There is. As I said before the parties come to terms, and the play is produced in England, it is a success; supposing I am the proprietor of it here, I am also its owner in America, and I deal with it in the United States just as I do here. If it is a manager or actor or other person who has bought it and they come to me I act as their agent for America; they could not secure the advantages accruing in the United States except through a United States citizen, and it is not out of place to mention in evidence of the correctness of our transactions between the French and English authors that the Dramatic Authors Society have made us their sole and exclusive agents."

"What is the process of securing a French author's rights?"

"That is a very important question and it also applies to English authors securing American rights. When the French author has come to terms he must print his play—not publish it mark you, print it—print a literal translation in English, within three months; he must register a transfer of the piece to the English purchaser, in order to bring the title into an English register and transfer book."

"The English proprietor must register at Stationers' Hall, I presume?"

"Yes, but he must not publish it, in the ordinary sense, for this is held to be a dedication to the public."

"I quite understand. Now, previous to your dealings in dramatic copyright—I mean in regard to these transactions between France, England and America—how did the authors fare?"

"They got very little for their works in the United States; $500 was considered quite a large sum, for the reason that there was nobody on the other side to take an interest in protecting their rights. But since we have taken this business up we have done for the author what he couldn't do for himself, we have worked and protected his property in a business way." . . .

"While benefiting your own house, you hold then, you are a benefactor to authors?" —"Certainly I do. Take the 'Celebrated Case' as an example. It was played over 100 nights in New York; we paid the author in France several thousand dollars; it was infringed upon by Gilmore in Baltimore; we protected it, and a decision in our favour. By this success we and others are enabled to make handsome offers to French authors for other plays."

"Who adapted the 'Celebrated Case' for America?"

"A New York author."

"To what English authors have you paid most for American representations?"

"Byron, Gilbert and Wills."

"For what pieces most?"

" 'Our Boys', 'Charity' and 'Olivia'."

"To whom have you paid most?"

"Byron."

"May I ask you what you have paid him in fees for 'Our Boys'?"

"Over $5,000."

"Now, Mr French, without reference to any present litigation what is your view of the condition of the law of copyright between England and America; I mean in this respect, how must an English author protect himself in America?"

"He can only do so through an American citizen, and although copyright law has actually been denied by some American lawyers, it has been established in the courts by our greatest Judges—Story, Blackstone, Cadwallader, Sprague, Nelson, Abbott, Woodbury and others; but a play must not be published; manuscript is sacred; publication is a dedication to the public. There is a nice point whether a person remembering a play may not use it as if it were his own. But the *American Law Review* (excuse me referring to this, my memory does not serve me sufficiently as to the details), writing on a host of decisions, explains that the rights of an author of a drama in his composition are two-fold:

" 'He is entitled to the profits arising from its performance, and also from the sale of the manuscript or the printing and publishing it. . . .'

"And I don't see that a man is entitled to be blamed for legally defending his property whether it be a drama or a horse; all I ask is fair play and what the law allows and so far as the drama is concerned I am sure we shall have better pieces, and that authors of repute will be the more induced to write for the stage if their plays are honourably protected in their interests."

"That is not an answer to any question I have asked."

"No, but you will oblige me by accepting it. I don't want to take up anything that has been said about me or my transaction, but I defy anyone to say my record is not patently straight and that this business is not conducted on fair, honest principles of plain simple deals."

As the century drew to its close Wentworth Hogg came to play a bigger and bigger part in the business. In 1893 Samuel French married Ada Emily, widow of Major Astley-Sparke of Norfolk. It was his second marriage, his first wife having died in 1887. At the same time the London business was turned into a limited company. Ada Emily received a dowry of £10,000, which was just about everything French possessed, and the £30,000 worth of shares that had been issued to form the company were deposited with her trustees as security against an income of £1,000 to be paid to her out of the profits of the business during her lifetime.

By the time French died in 1898 at the age of 77, Wentworth Hogg had built up strong personal friendships with the authors and was carrying the goodwill of the business in his own person. This was fortunate because, to quote Wentworth Hogg's words:

"*Sometime before Mr French's second marriage he developed a kind of mania for patents by getting connected with a man named Plumb . . . A considerable sum of money was lost through this man inducing French to invest in such mad schemes as a Patent process for making 4d worth of butter into 1/6d worth. Then there was the patent gold paint, and the gold cure for drunkeness, also the asthma cure, and patent glove stretchers, and insulators.*"

As more and more of his savings disappeared, French (and presumably poor Wentworth Hogg) became so nervous about the state of affairs that he eventually made an agreement with Hogg that he would not enter into any further speculations without the consent of the latter. When French's health finally broke down, he wisely left everything in the hands of Wentworth Hogg.

By the turn of the century, amateur interest in acting had increased enormously. Amateur dramatic groups began to take their leisure activity rather more seriously, and the light-hearted tolerance of mishaps chronicled by the *Hairdressers' Trade Journal* gradually vanished away. Wentworth Hogg concentrated on building up this aspect of the business rather than the professional (but did not ignore the latter altogether), and in an article published around the turn of the century, he described how the firm had expanded to cope with the growth of amateur interest:

"*When I first began with Mr French, an office boy, an old housekeeper, Mr French and myself were the staff. We used to get about a hundred letters during the busiest part of the season, and flattered ourselves that we were on the high road to prosperity. Now our first post frequently brings us five hundred letters, and, besides other officials, seven shorthand clerks have as much as they can do to keep pace with the correspondence. The stock season and the stock*

8

theatre were the great attractions in those early times, and much of the work was in manuscript only. Then came into fashion the amateur and the amateur club and the touring companies for London, all of which created a demand for the printed play. I mention the amateur first simply because he is the one who wants the printed dramatist—he is our greatest patron. Even when he may not be playing he likes to read, and consequently to purchase the new plays and the pieces with which he is familiar. And, as you know, from the amateur comes the professional. The earnest amateur is the backbone of the stage, because he means well, and wants to do well from every point of view."

Mr Hogg gave further insight into how the firm had grown in another interview published around the same time in the *Penny Pictorial Magazine*: "*To keep up the stock we have to print on an average fifty thousand plays a month. That means six hundred thousand a year, so our printing bill is a heavy one.*"

His figures however have a suspect air about them, and should not be taken too literally. French himself had not been above exaggeration, and had once talked of having six million books in the place—a figure that is palpably absurd. On another occasion he talked of having paid £15,000 for the rights of a single play. As he only paid £5,000 for the whole of Lacy's business this requires more than a grain of salt to give it credence.

It was not only the interests of the amateurs that Wentworth Hogg looked after, but also those of the authors of the plays, collecting the performing fees for all who placed themselves under the Samuel French banner. He fought the Dramatic Authors' Society when it tried to undercut his rates of commission, but which was not able to offer the same degree of service.

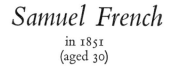

Samuel French
in 1851
(aged 30)

Meanwhile in America the business of Samuel French & Son was developing alongside the Theatres as they both worked their way steadily up-town as New York expanded. There is some doubt about the exact date when French started to publish plays under his own name. He is reported to have stated that the venture began in 1854 at 151 Nassau Street, but there is evidence that he was publishing as early as 1846 from 293 Broadway. It may have been that the publications prior to 1854 were not plays. He moved from Broadway to Nassau Street in 1850. At that time 45th Street, where the present offices are, was still farmland, and the theatres were clustered round lower Broadway, south of the Bowery. The population of the city was then about half-a-million, but over the next twenty years it was to double in size as the city expanded northwards taking the theatres with it.

Mem^d. of agreement made this 13th day of February 1890 Between Geoge Alexander (for himself and Hamilton Aide) of the one part and Samuel French, of the other part.

1. The said S. French to pay to the said parties of the one part the sum of £250. on account and by way of payment in advance of ~~any~~ their share of any fees to be hereafter received by him in respect of working the Comedy "Dr. Bill" in North America (including the United States and Canada &c)

2. The said S. French to take the usual and necessary steps for securing all American rights in the said play, and the parties of the one part to execute all necessary assignments to him requisite to enable him to legally secure such ~~rights~~ American rights. He further undertaking to use his best endeavours to promote the representations of the said piece and to obtain the best terms in his power by way of fees or royalties.

3. The said S. French to have and retain for his own use absolutely One third of the net profits arising therefrom and to punctually account for and pay the remaining Two third

2

share thereof (after first deducting and retaining the said advance of £250.) monthly a oftener when received by him to the said G. Alexander and H. Aidé.

4. The said parties of the one part undertaking not to permit the said Play to be published by printing in England or to do or permit any other act invalidating the American rights.

5. To furnish the said S. French with complete M.S. of Play, music, models or sketches of scenery, scene and property, plots samples of all printing, and also to furnish him from time to time with true copies of any amendments alterations or additions that may be made at any time hereafter in said Play

Received as for above contract £250.

Feb. 13th 90   Hamilton Aidé.
Geo. Alexander:
                        Saml French

Contract between Samuel French and George Alexander and Hamilton Aidé for the exploitation of
Dr Bill in America. The play had been adapted by Aidé from the French *Le Docteur Jo-Jo* of Albert
Carré. Performed in Paris in March 1888, and in London at the Court Theatre in December 1894.
It was played in America in a version by Oscar Barrett under the title *The Kangaroo Girl*.

French stayed in Nassau Street, moving to 121 and 122, until 1878 when he followed the theatres up-town and took premises at 38 East 14th Street, close to Union Square, at that time the centre of theatrical activity. The theatres were there; the dramatic agencies were there; and, nearby, were the homes of many of the actors, actresses and authors. There were then twenty-eight theatres in New York and Entertainment was about to become Big Business.

The next moves occurred in 1887 and 1896 when, in response to a new theatrical focus that was forming around Washington Square, French's moved to 22nd Street, first to No 19 and later to Nos 24 & 26. Another stop came in 1910 at 28 West 38th Street as the theatres reached the famous 42nd Street and Times Square. Since then theatres have been built still further up-town, with a few stragglers even reaching as far as Central Park, and the last move, in 1924, took French's to their present address at 25 West 45th Street.

Thomas Henry French had been twenty-four years old when his father had left him in sole charge of the New York business in 1872. Six years later the *Washington Capitol* described him as:
"*. . . the theatrical entrepreneur, with a highly coloured face and gold-rimmed eye-glasses. He is interested in the success of both "Diplomacy" and "A Celebrated Case", and he wanders in every evening to count the house and the profits that accrue. He is a generous liver, a widower, and gives dinner parties, breakfast parties, supper parties, theatre parties galore . . .*"
His clothes were rich and tasteful and he was very much the man about town. In the late 1880s and early nineties he was leasing and managing the old Grand Opera House on 8th Avenue and 23rd Street, and with Frank W Sanger was also running the Broadway Theatre. When the newly built Garden Theatre was added to the Madison Square Garden complex, in 1890, Thomas Henry and Samuel appeared on the bills as joint managers. In 1893 he built and managed the America Theatre, one of the first to appear on 42nd Street. The theatre specialized in lavishly staged extravaganzas. It also had the distinction of having a second theatre on the roof reached by the then novel means of an elevator. Unfortunately in 1897 he lost control as the result of a foreclosure judgement.

For a while he was lessee and manager of the New Park Theatre, and a rather curious paragraph in *The World* in 1878 says, "*Thomas H. French took that kind of leave of the Park Theatre as co-proprietor because the elder French in London thought management incompatible with their relations to authors, playwrights and the profession generally.*" This is difficult to reconcile with the Frenchs' continued involvement in management throughout the next two decades. The Park Theatre, which had been built in 1874 for Dion Boucicault and was burnt down in 1882, had been an "Unlucky House" and one possible reason for the "excuse" may have been that French did not want to admit that he was getting out due to financial losses there.

A factor that was of great importance to the Frenchs was the development of the Railroads. Hitherto the country outside of New York had been dependent on Stock Companies for their theatre; with visiting actors of note joining them from time to time for special performances. But as the Railroads inched their ways across the country it became possible to send out tours of metropolitan productions, and Samuel and his son were not slow to take advantage of this new facility. They were in a very good position to do so.

Although performance rights had been granted to playwrights by an amendment to the 1846 Copyright Act they proved to be virtually unenforceable. The Frenchs, however, had some advantage over other managements as Samuel in England was able to acquire the American rights of many English and continental plays, and Thomas Henry, as an American citizen was able to exploit them. In 1878 he was one of those who tried to get a new proprietory rights bill through Congress:
"*. . . That the law of copyright shall cover and protect managers, actors and other citizens of the United States who shall procure through purchase the right to a play, be it farce, comedy, tragedy, drama or spectacular representation, from a foreign author, for the purpose of playing or publishing the same in the United States . . .*"
But pressure was brought to bear against the Bill which was considered to have been framed solely in their own interests, to serve their private fortunes. He was more fortunate, however, in getting a favourable judgement in the Courts over the rights in leasing plays. It was not until 1891, when the Chase Act was

passed, no doubt with backing from the Frenchs, that protection was at last generally extended to foreigners.

The 1880s were probably Thomas Henry French's heyday. In addition to his productions in New York he was sending first-rate companies on extensive tours. He also toured the Lillian Russell Opera Company, and for a time his name was associated with the lady's. With Frank W Sanger he sent out four companies simultaneously in *Little Lord Fauntleroy*. But this last was not entirely a happy venture and was vexed with disputes, and he ended up with a judgement against him for $68,000. Nevertheless, it was *Little Lord Fauntleroy* that set the American business firmly on its feet.

There was always a lot of traffic in plays between the New York and the London ends of the business, but as the 1890s progressed this traffic across the Atlantic became unbalanced as Thomas Henry imported large quantities of books and failed to pay for them. This was a source of great worry and concern to Wentworth Hogg.

> "For what with us began simply as a business has, through the expenditure of many thousands of dollars, long years of hard work, day and night, with the co-operation of an able, experienced, and enthusiastic staff of associates, developed into an institution, affecting the lives, happiness and education of a nation."

It was the London end of the business that developed the idea of controlling the performing rights and the collection of royalties on them. Samuel acquired not only the publishing rights but also the rights of performance of plays throughout the British Isles, later adding the same rights for America. Authors no doubt began to see the great advantages to be gained by having the wider distribution that could be given through printed copies selling on both sides of the Atlantic coupled with a system that controlled performances and collected royalties.

Thomas Henry French died in December 1902; only four years after his father. The London end of the business was now bought by Wentworth Hogg; and the New York by a partnership headed by Thomas R Edwards, who had been closely associated in it with Thomas Henry since the 1880s. This separation into two financially independent firms did not affect the co-operation that had always existed between London and New York. Information, rights and stock continued to be exchanged across the Atlantic, though no doubt on a much more business-like basis. London, one can imagine, continued to talk about its "New York branch" and New York to refer to its "little branch in London".

Edwards may have lacked the Theatrical aura and the reputation of man-about-town of his predecessor, but his business instincts were sounder. A delightful story is told that he was a great friend of the police, who all knew him. He always carried a roll of dollar bills, and travelled to the theatre in a chauffeur-driven Rolls. He always alighted at the same place on 5th Avenue, and there would be a policeman

From *The World* April 12, 1878

The dramatic agencies of Wall or Simmons and the publishing house of French & Son sustain, perhaps, the most important relations to things and persons dramatic, because their business ramifies throughout the States and over Europe. . . .

When one considers there are more than two hundred thousand people actively and constantly connected with places of theatrical amusements . . . it is at once recognized how important people are Messrs. Wall or Simmons and many agents like them in this and other cities. Similar considerations also will explain the magnitude to which the business of Samuel French & Son has grown. Indeed, they practically monopolize the business selling, negotiating, printing, copyrighting and supervising plays in this country and in England. In London the firm succeeded the well-known Lacy, and the house in which the business is transacted is quite a feature in the west part of the Strand at the foot of the Bedford Street hill that is crowned by the sparkling glass-roof of Covent Garden Market abutting on the old theatre and present Opera House. . . .

Probably £20,000 are invested in the business. Not an insignificant part of it is under the custom of amateurs from all portions of the United Kingdom who desire scenery ordered or materials for make-up, and all varieties of stage appointments, in which the firm also deal.

The New York home is under management of Thomas H French, the son, and who is also agent for many British, German and French authors who prefer to keep their dramas in manuscripts and peddle out stage rights—a species of quasi international copyright which the courts have yet definitely to countenance; although there can be no doubt that an author or his assignee can protect a complete transfer of manuscript as an entirety, the doubt hinging upon the multiplication of copies for representation by many owners. The stores corner of University Place and Union Square are not yet fully in order, but the same kind of business will be done there as in London. . . .

The firm removed from a Nassau Street third-story, where about thirty years ago the elder French (who, by the way, is a Yankee entitled to wear the Mayflower in his *boutonnière*) began business in a modest way.

waiting to whom he would give a dollar bill. Years later, his grandson, going to the theatre, found himself invited to park outside. Those were the days! It was during Edwards' time that the New York office began to publish the principal contemporary American plays, whereas before it had been mainly very light European dramas and farces that had found their way into print. People were quite happy to perform such plays in their parlours or in church halls, and the whole business of amateur theatricals was regarded as a fairly harmless pastime, as long as it was material of this kind that was being produced; it had not been very many years before that a really good play had been looked upon as an instrument of evil and the production of plays as rather dangerous in many parts of the United States. Gradually, however,

amateur groups began to take a much keener and more critical interest in the material that was available to them. An awareness that the old slapstick farces and popular French and German dramas were not really worthy of their time and effort began to dawn, and the demand for more worthwhile and relevant plays grew. This demand was met by the "better" plays that Edwards began to issue around this time— plays ranging from the classics of Aristophanes and Terence to the work of contemporary American authors. It was a timely move, for the best of these soon became known to amateurs, and as the quality and quantity of available plays improved, so the number of amateur groups increased. It was now that the amateur side of the business really began to develop, as the seeds of the Little Theatre movement were sown. By the time of the 1914–18 war, such groups, along with the High School societies, were the firm's best customers.

Edwards' three partners were Frank J Sheil, Frank Stevens and Henry Staton, a lawyer. When Edwards died in 1930 Sheil took over. It was in the years of the Depression and Sheil nursed the business through with a series of budget plays such as *Aunt Tilly Goes to Town* and *Lily the Felon's Daughter*, light escapist material that matched the need and pockets of the time. The upturn came at the end of the decade with *Our Town*, still the most popular and successful play of the present century in the States. Sheil was followed by Stevens in 1946, and in 1952 Edwards' grandson M Abbott Van Nostrand took over. Mr Van Nostrand is still the head of the business, now on both sides of the Atlantic as chairman of the New York and the London offices.

The first directors of Samuel French Ltd had been French himself, Wentworth Hogg, and a solicitor named Muskerry Tilson. At their first meeting they appointed A W Boughton as auditor, fixing his fee at five guineas. A dividend of 10 per cent was declared out of a net profit of £3,549 6s 9d. Mr Boughton's name is worthy of mention because although his firm has changed its name several times and there have been a number of amalgamations with other accountants, it is his successors who continue to be our auditors to this day. Tilson, who had dabbled on his own account in acquiring dramatic copyrights, died in June 1918, and Wentworth Hogg's son Cyril (b 1885) was appointed a director in his place.

After the War, Wentworth Hogg gradually eased himself out of the business, and by the early 1920s had retired to live in Brighton, leaving his son in sole charge. It is largely to Cyril Hogg that we owe the present success and high standing of the business today. His interest in the theatre, professional and amateur, was intense, and his standards were exacting.

Nineteen Twenty saw the beginning of the Literary and Dramatic Agencies as we know them today. Previously authors had handled their own plays: they placed them, struck their own bargains, and managed their own affairs. Wentworth Hogg had dealt directly with his authors; his son soon found himself dealing with middlemen. This was among the first of many changes in a developing Theatre to which he would have to adjust during the next forty-odd years.

The Theatre of the 1920s and 1930s was largely one of fashionable entertainment. Audiences expected plays to have three different sets and the cast three different changes of costumes to prevent them becoming bored. Plays tended to be on the shallow side; not to provoke too much thought or controversy. That is not to say there were no serious writers in the theatre; indeed there were those who believed it was the Theatre's job to instruct not to amuse. But plays of substance were not so thick on the ground that they could occupy more than a handful of London's fifty-eight theatres at any one time. It was also a period when there could be as many as three Companies touring the same light play in the provinces at the same time.

Cyril Hogg had an instinctive understanding of the needs of the theatre, and was always ready with a helping hand wherever it was needed. He enjoyed entertaining and built lasting friendships with both authors and agents. He would buy a play, even though he knew it could lose money, if he could see some merit in it and felt it ought to be published.

In 1936 he fought the case known as Jennings v Stephens that clarified the legal distinction between public performances and those that were private and domestic under the Copyright Act, thereby establishing a code of practice which has helped to safeguard authors' rights ever since.

By 1950 a number of companies that complimented the play publishing business and served the needs of theatrical entertainment, both stage and film, had been brought together in one group. It included the costumiers B J Simmons and Charles H Fox, the armourers and jewellers Robert White, Fashion Hire who supplied modern costumes, A & L Corne makers of hats and caps, the English & French Embroidery Co, and Stage Scenery who specialized in hiring sets for the use of amateur operatic societies. For many years Simmons was a source of pride to Cyril Hogg. The fact that the business was not profitable was irrelevant to him. "Some rich men run racehorses," he once said, "I run a Theatrical Costumiers as a hobby."

But like other empires this one suffered the wind of change. For the most part the products were too good, and the cost of the craftsmanship in producing authentic costumes and transporting the scenery used and designed for West End productions were too high for a market that was being forced to modify its standards. Of all these companies only Charles H Fox and Robert White survive today, the former still hiring costumes and being the principal outlet for Stage Make-Up in this country, and the latter specializing in Armour and replicas of the Crown Jewels as well as Stage Jewellery.

Among the many changes that Cyril Hogg had to adapt to were the disappearance of the old Actor-Manager and the rise of the Theatrical Entrepreneur and the big Producing Managements; the increasing liberality of the Lord Chamberlain's licence in the 1950s, which was not to his liking; and the replacement of authors who wrote "well-made" plays that he understood by the new school who scorned the classic mould and were seeking a new vigour.

With the death of Cyril Hogg in February 1964 another era in the narrative of French's in London came to an end. Lacy, French and the Hoggs are the legends behind us: the chronicle of the last decade and a half is too recent to be reviewed in perspective. Suffice it to say it has been a period of great growth.

In America, the Stock companies, including the League of Regional Theatres, which were almost killed off by the coming of the Talkies, cruelly followed by the Depression, are once more flourishing again, and form a vital part of the business; so too are the Little Theatres; and more recently has come the development of the Dinner Theatre which is proving increasingly popular.

The emphasis in Britain has been more on the Theatre Bookshop offering a well-informed specialist service which now covers the English-speaking World, and many foreign-speaking countries as well, to an extent our predecessors never imagined.

Cyril Hogg was followed by his son Anthony; at the same time Harold F Dyer who for many years had looked after the Musical Plays, became Managing Director. In 1975 he retired and the British and American firms merged, bringing them once again under unified control after a separation of seventy-seven years.

In 1980 our services are available from Offices in New York, London, Hollywood, Toronto and Sydney; and from Agencies in Wellington (New Zealand), Cape Town, Johannesburg, Singapore, Valletta (Malta), Salisbury (Rhodesia), and Nairobi (Kenya).

My host received me in his private study, a large room on the first floor, commanding a good view of the bustling Strand and the slight ascent of Southampton Street, and decorated with many portraits and pictures of theatrical interest.

"I should like to begin our conversation by showing you over the entire premises," said Mr. French, and crossing the room, he swung open a wide, sliding door of iron, let into the wall, of which it looked a veritable part. A great recess, or cupboard, stood revealed. "This," said Mr. French, "is our 'safe.' Stored here you see the manuscripts of some two thousand plays and operas which are not printed or published, and of which the rights are protected only by the equity law of stage rights." Mr. French then escorted me over the rest of the first floor. I stopped on the way to admire the winding staircase.

"Yes," said Mr. French, "the old house takes us back to the spacious days of Great Elizabeth. The fabric has hardly been altered at all. "See here," and he indicated a brass plate on the first landing, whereon I read: "This building was erected in order that the Aldermen of the City of London might witness from its windows Queen Elizabeth drive by, on her way to be crowned."

We then ascended and explored the three floors above, glancing, in turn, through a work-room devoted chiefly to the stitching of wrappers, a sanctum occupied by such mysteries as wigs, make-up materials, grease-paints, tableau-lights, &c.; and a recess with Mr. French's well-known fit-up proscenium and set of stock scenery for the use of amateurs, in full working order.

"I am quite proud of this miniature scenic arrangement," said Mr. French. "It has an enormous popularity with amateurs all over the country." And he proceeded to show me the various possible changes of scene, which include a drawing-room set, a cottage, a wood, a garden, and all else that the heart of the amateur can desire.

"In this and my various other descriptive catalogues," said Mr. French, handing me an illustrated pamphlet, "lies half the secret of the far-reaching connection which I have established for my business."

I looked at the pamphlet, and found that it contained the most elaborately complete instructions for the arrangement of this model stage and its fittings. Mr. French's catalogues must, indeed, be a boon to the professional and the amateur alike, for they are a marvel of minute information, including summaries of plots, directions for dresses, and scales of fees for performance. The Robertson plays, I find, have a catalogue "on their own," giving a detailed analysis of their plots, scenery, length in playing, and original casts—altogether, a most interesting souvenir. The copyright of the set was bought for £5000. That this sum was invested to good advantage one may safely conclude. Another bend of the staircase brought us to the top floor.

"Here," said my host, "lie the residue of the theatrical publications of Duncan and Cumberland, and of Lacy's 'Acting Editions,' of which I took over the stock. There repose the manuscripts of most of Boucicault's plays, and in the next room we keep unbound stock, and MSS. of plays not printed, but let out on hire."

Having briefly explored the upper regions of this home of dramatic literature, we descended to the cellars beneath the ground floor.

"Here," said Mr. French, "is my real storehouse—my bank. Tons of stereotyped plates rest here. From this reservoir we replenish our stock. Here are plays of the Elizabethan age cheek by jowl with modern farcical comedies—alphabetical arrangement makes strange bedfellows!"

THE CELLARS AND VAULTS.

It is here, far below the level of the street, that the stereotyped pages of the plays are stored.

Our Buildings

Comparatively little is known about 17 Wellington Street or 89 The Strand. Neither building appears to have had any particular architectural merit, or to have housed any distinguished persons. Wellington Street was not built until after the English Opera House was burnt down in 1830; but 89 The Strand was undoubtedly much older, though nothing like as old as the three hundred years that the *New York Times* reported. If we were to divide by two we would probably be nearer the mark.

In 1900 The Strand was widened, No. 89 was pulled down, and French's moved to its present address, 26 Southampton Street, a building of considerable historic and architectural interest. This and the next door house, No. 27, are the only two original buildings left in the street. Both were built in 1708 on ground that had been part of the garden of Bedford House. From 1931 to 1974 we occupied the greater part of No. 27 as well, but we now use only the basement, which still has its original well with a lead water tank above it.

The Abbots of Westminster had owned the ground that came to be known as *The Convent Garden* from soon after 1200 AD until the Reformation three hundred years later. It served conveniently both as burial ground and as kitchen garden, and their surplus of fresh vegetables were eagerly bought by the ever-hungry populace of London from the other side of the Temple Bar. At the Dissolution of the Monasteries the ground had been given to the Duke of Somerset, but on his attainder in 1552 John Russell, Earl of Bedford, became the owner of the seven acres bounded by The Strand on the south and the Long Acre on the north.

The Russells built themselves "a large but old-built house, with a spacious garden, having a terrace-walk adjoining to the brick wall next to the garden, behind which were coach houses and stables, with a conveyance into Charles St, through a large gate". Bedford House, as it was called, stood where Southampton Street now joins The Strand, and the gardens were bounded on the north side by a wall that ran from what is now Henrietta Street towards Bow Street. Queen Anne had recently come to the throne when the Russells inherited, through marriage with the Southamptons, an estate in Bloomsbury. The Tudor mansion in The Strand was no longer needed, and by 1704 the garden wall, the trees, and the house had all vanished. By 1708 new houses had sprung up on Bedford Ground, and a road, named after the Southamptons, linked them to The Strand. A bar closed it to all but privileged traffic. It was not until 1860 that the Gate Keeper's lodge was removed.

In the new street, No. 31 was occupied by Ambrose Godfrey, the oldest manufacturing chemist in London, who had started business in 1584 and endured until 1860. His premises ran through into Maiden Lane. Also in Maiden Lane was "The Bedford Head", a tavern that is sometimes described as being in Southampton Street, and is not to be confused with "The Bedford Arms" which was "the second house east of Southampton Street on the south-east side of Covent Garden".

Covent Garden was the nursery of eighteenth-century English culture. All the best known names in Art, Music and Literature in the seventeenth and eighteenth centuries were to be found in the immediate vicinity. Colley Cibber was born in a house on Bedford Ground at the northern end of Southampton Street. Congreve lived there: Addison, Steele, Pope, Otway, Butler were all living nearby. So too were the doctors Arne and Johnson. Kneller and Lely had studios in the Piazza built by Inigo Jones, so also did Hogarth. Quin was born in King Street, Booth and Wilkes lived in Bow Street. And at No. 8 Russell Street Johnson first met Boswell.

Sheridan fought his famous duel with Matthews for the honour of Miss Linley (also local born) at "The Castle Tavern" in Henrietta Street. Round the corner in Maiden Lane, Andrew Marvell lived next door to "The Bedford Head", and two doors away at the sign of "The White Peruke" Voltaire lodged for a while after his sojourn in the Bastille.

19

The best known inhabitant of Southampton Street was undoubtedly David Garrick. He had been married to the dancer Eva Marie Violetta in June 1749, and it was to No. 27 that he brought his bride. Garrick was then 32 and his wife 25. He had been a successful actor for no more than ten years, after being an unsuccessful wine merchant, but he must have become a man of considerable substance to have afforded a four-storey brick built house with thirteen spacious rooms with panelled walls and a basement. It is likely too that the plaster ceilings of the principal rooms were decoratively painted like those of 26 next door. Garrick spent the greater part of his working life in this house on Bedford Ground, not leaving it until 1772 when he went to live in Adelphi Terrace. We are told: "he did not find it so well suited to him as the warm and sheltered apartments in Southampton Street."

There is a story told that Garrick invited Dr Johnson to breakfast one day at No. 27. The two had travelled together from Lichfield to London some twelve years earlier, with but a few pence in their pockets. The Doctor was entertained in a room at the top of the house, and all the way up the stairs the doors were left open so that he might see the splendour in which Davy now lived. Garrick had acquired the house through the good offices of the Wyndham family who had occupied it between 1720 and 1737. It was a relative of Lady Wyndham's who became the daughter-in-law of Lord Milton who was for a while her next-door neighbour at No. 26.

*On Thursday Mr Damer supped at the Bedford Arms, in Covent Garden, with four ladies and a blind fiddler. At three in the morning he dismissed his seraglio, ordering his Orpheus to come up again in half an hour. When he returned he found his master dead, and smelt gunpowder. He called; the master of the house came up; and they found Mr Damer sitting in a chair dead, with one pistol beside him and another in his pocket. The ball had not gone through his head or made any report. On the table lay a scrap of paper with these words—*The people of the house are not to blame for what has happened; it was my own act . . .—*What a catastrophe for a man at thirty-two, heir to two-and-twenty thousand a year! Five thousand a year in present and* £22,000 *in reversion, are not, it would seem, sufficient for happiness and cannot check a pistol.* (Horace Walpole)

This tragedy took place in 1776 when Mr Damer, son of Lord Milton (later Earl of Dorchester) found that his father would not pay his debts of £70,000. After his death his wardrobe was sold for £15,000! His wife (or should we say widow?) was the fashionable sculptress Anne Seymour Damer, who was later to inherit Walpole's home, Strawberry Hill.

By the end of the eighteenth century, Covent Garden was beginning to lose its glitter as a place to live in. At night it was unsafe for pedestrians to be abroad, and the Watch—aged, infirm, unsober, and popularly known as "Charlies"—were powerless against the Mohocks, who broke their halberds and frequently locked them in their own stand-boxes.

After 1800, No. 27 became just another commercial building; first an hotel and then offices. No. 26 had ceased to be a private dwelling in 1745.

In the more leisurely days of Victorian/Edwardian England what Mr Hogg and the *Penny Pictorial* considered busy would hardly make a ripple on our equanimity today. Great pains were taken when we moved to Southampton Street to create more of a Reading Room than a Bookshop for the comfort of those wanting to choose plays for performance. But the atmosphere of the place is very special to us and we have guarded it jealously. There is still something of the quality of the eighteenth century even today.

A VIEW OF THE INTERIOR.
Here can be purchased almost any play of note ever produced on the stage.

THE PLAY SHOP
THE ONLY BUSINESS OF ITS KIND IN THE WORLD

Few passing through that historic thorough-fare, the Strand, can fail to notice the play shop. Its exterior at once attracts attention, calls, in fact, aloud for notice; notwith-standing that the frontage has been largely rebuilt, the imprint of age has not been effaced, there is still an ancient look about it. Moreover, the window is one which has no companion between Temple Bar and Charing Cross.

Into no other shop can you go and ask for a play—drama, comedy, farce—any play from Shakespeare's "Julius Caesar" to almost the latest London success, and get your requirements satisfied; French's are the only people in England who can oblige you. They keep 6,000 plays on hand.

from *The Penny Pictorial Magazine*, 10th January 1901

The Play Shop in the 1970s

Our Authors

Most people collect something whether it be stamps or match-boxes, old masters or paper-clips. Publishers collect Authors. But whereas stamps and old masters can be expected to become more valuable with age, Authors tend to go out of copyright, die and refuse to write any more. Some years ago however we were approached by a woman who claimed to be the amanuensis to a whole host of Authors from beyond the Styx. Part of her life was spent in a trance while they dictated their new plays to her. It was not at all clear what sort of contract we could expect to have with the Authors nor how their royalties were to be transmitted to them. Presumably they would have had no problems monitoring infringements of their copyrights, and would have saved us a good deal of expense; but generally we did not feel that this indestructible body of playwrights would be able to adapt to the changing moods and styles of contemporary Theatre. At the risk of losing some immortal works we turned down this playwriter.

No Publisher can be better than his Authors, who are after all his only asset. We have been fortunate to have been associated with almost all the best, and best known, playwrights in our 150 years. Some like Shakespeare were dead before we were thought of, and out of copyright, and therefore had no say in the matter, but many, many, more chose to be published by French's. It is a long list, currently running to several hundred names on our books. But quantity means little: names like Robert Bolt and Alan Bennett, Peter Shaffer, Alan Ayckbourn, Tom Stoppard and Harold Pinter are more significant. Messrs Waterhouse & Hall, Brooke & Bannerman, Ted Willis and David Wood all contribute to the varied fare we can offer from our list today. So too do William Douglas Home, Michael Frayn, Neil Simon and James Saunders. But where does one stop when one is dropping names? One cannot leave out John Mortimer or Ronald Millar; Bill Naughton, Peter Nichols, Alan Pater and David Storey must be included, so too must John Bowen, Constance Cox and Brian Clemens. Working backwards we must not forget Jean Anouilh and J B Priestley, Noël Coward and Terence Rattigan, and in lighter vein Philip King. Then there were those other masters of the ridiculous Vernon Sylvaine and Ben Travers (happily he is still with us); the wisdom and stylish dialogue of Enid Bagnold and the poetry and vigour of Clemence Dane; and those marvellous translations into the twentieth century of Molière by Miles Malleson. The social comments on the upper classes by Frederick Lonsdale were followed by the middle class comments of Dodie Smith, Esther McCracken and R F Delderfield, and later by the social satire of Arthur Macrae. Earlier were the plays of Sean O'Casey and J M Synge, which are still performed today and rate as classics.

Among the Americans the comedy writer Neil Simon is the obvious leader, and like Edward Albee, with his deep insight into the human condition, is popular on both sides of the Atlantic; while the appeal of Woody Allen and Jerry Herman is mostly among their compatriots. James Baldwin, Bernard Slade and David Mamet are also of considerable stature in their own country.

The plays of Thornton Wilder, with his strongly Christian view of Good and Evil in Man, are very much alive today. Less so perhaps are those of Elmer Rice, experimental in their time, and challenging in their ideas. Both of them authors of work that travelled well to Europe. In lighter vein are the comedies of Jerome Lawrence & Robert E Lee.

Harold Brighouse is still remembered for *Hobson's Choice*, and Barrie is still admired as a superb craftsman, but other names from the earlier part of this century may go unrecognized by many younger people. H M Harwood, Ian Hay and Walter Hackett (who built the Whitehall Theatre for his wife); Ronald Jeans, Dion Titheradge and the Farjeons, the masters of the Revue Sketch, and Israel Zangwill, ring fewer bells than they should. Bridging the nineteenth and twentieth centuries is the remarkable Arthur Wing Pinero who wrote 75 plays of which 54 were produced between 1877 and 1932. A fine craftsman, he managed to absorb all the changes of style through the Victorian, Edwardian and early Georgian years.

How many people today remember the other Authors who bridged the two centuries; Alfred Sutro, R C Carton and J H McCarthy; Haddon Chambers, Sydney Grundy, and Henry Arthur Jones? All were popular in their time, but with the exception of Jones they have not worn all that well.

It comes as a slight shock to find that Oscar Wilde (1856–1900) was wholly Victorian. We think of *The Importance of Being Earnest* as a play of Today and not as one written only fifteen years short of a century ago. And behind him, in a more shadowy past, are Blanchard and Dion Boucicault, and the early plays of W S Gilbert; H J Byron and Planché the writers of Extravaganzas and hideous puns, Oxenford and Mark Lemon and the reformer T W Robertson, *et al.*

No mention has been made of the many writers of One-Act Plays who sustained the Amateur Drama with a constant supply of new material which we published in the years between the wars, and after, but for which there is now less demand. Gertrude Jennings, Philip Johnson, L du Garde Peach, T B Morris, Mabel Constanduros, and more recently Norman Holland and Margaret Wood, are names that come to mind, and must carry the banner for the many others, and for the earlier writers who supplied One-Act Plays in the days when audiences, accustomed to long sermons in church, demanded Curtain Raisers in the Theatre.

We have mentioned only a few of the many Authors to whom we owe our 150 years of successful existence—without them and all the others there could have been no French's.

A list of the Authors whose work is reprinted in our current London and New York catalogue appears on pages 35–40.

To Shriek or not to Shriek!

Today's authors, whose language is closer to the vernacular than ever before, intuitively adopt a rhetorical style of punctuation. This was not always so, and at one period our authors made free use of the Exclamation Mark. They seemed to have the mistaken idea that it injected emotion into what had been written. One of them went so far as to end every sentence in all his plays with!. We are happy to be able to report that he never noticed that we removed every single one of them—at least he never even put one back. Perhaps he never read his proofs!

TREDEGAR PARK THEATRE.

Under the Management of Mr. MORGAN, of Tredegar.

Stage Manager - - - - - - - - . Hon. R. BOURKE.

POSITIVELY FOR ONE NIGHT ONLY.

On FRIDAY EVENING, the 7th of January, 1853, will be performed by particular desire, the Amusing Farce by ALFRED WIGAN, Esq., of a

MODEL
FOR
A WIFE.

Mr. Stump, (Painter, and Teacher of Drawing)................MAJOR GEORGE MUNDY, (33rd Regt.)
Tom...HON. R. BOURKE.
Pygmalion Bonefoi.................................Mr. MORGAN, (of Tredegar.)
Mrs. Stump..Miss MILMAN.
Clara, (her niece)...Miss OWEN.
Two Young Ladies (Stump's pupils).....Miss ELLEN and Miss GEORGINA MORGAN.

To be followed by a Coloured Sketch, called

'TAKING BY STORM.'

Backhuysen..................................Mr. MORGAN.
Tom Piper.......................................HON. A. HARDINGE.
Betsy Mizen...................................Miss E. MORGAN.
Fanny Sebright......................................Miss MORGAN.
Martha..Miss GEORGINA MORGAN.
Charity Girl...................................Miss MARY MORGAN.

LADY MORGAN and Miss JEMIMA MILMAN have kindly promised to perform the Overture, assisted by the Tredegar Harper.

Sir GEORGE WALKER, Bart. has also offered his valuable assistance on this occasion, and will sing by particular desire, in the interval between the pieces.

Box Keeper, Mr. GODFREY MORGAN, (17th Lancers.)
The Saloon and Refreshment room will be kept by Mr. FREDERIC MORGAN.

EVANS, PRINTER AND STATIONER, PUBLIC LIBRARY, 35, HIGH STREET, NEWPORT.

A MODEL OF A WIFE.

First performed at the Theatre Royal, Lyceum, (under the management of Mrs. Keeley,) on the 27th day of January, 1845.

Characters.

MR. STUMP (*a Painter and Teacher of Drawing*).................................. Mr. F. MATTHEWS.
TOM .... Mr. MEADOWS.
PYGMALION BONNEFOI (*an enthusiastic Frenchman*).............................. Mr. A. WIGAN.
MRS. STUMP .... Miss WALCOTT.
CLARA .... (*her niece*) .... Miss FAIRBROTHER.
Two Young Ladies, Stump's Pupils.

Costumes.

PYGMALION BONNEFOI.—Modern French suit complete, large hat.
MR. STUMP.—Morning gown—then plain blue coat, trousers, &c., grey hair.
TOM.—Jacket, apron, corduroy trousers, white stockings and shoes, red wig.
MRS. STUMP.—Elegant muslin morning gown, cap, &c.
CLARA.—White muslin morning dress. A bridal veil covering the whole figure, bridal wreath and bouquet of orange flowers.
Two PUPILS.—Plain morning dresses, shawls and bonnets.

Scenery and Properties.

SCENE.—An artist's chamber. (2nd Grooves) Door in centre, doors R. and L. 1 E. Window, L. U. E.

PROPERTIES.—Many pictures placed about the stage; pallet, brush, and mahl stick, paints; portrait of a lady on easel; picture leaning against wing, R.; two chairs by table, chair by easel, large arm chair in middle on castors; lay figure, elegantly dressed in white, seated in chair, with a large white veil over the head falling to the feet all round, a wreath of orange flowers round the head, and a bouquet in hand; table, L., with four chairs, drawing sketches and pencils for pupils, and writing materials; an Arab dress for Tom to take on.

A MODEL OF A WIFE.

SCENE.—*An Artist's Studio; writing materials; near the table an easel. At the back a slab and muller for grinding colours; C., before the window, a lay figure, dressed as a bride, with bouquet, wreath, and veil, seated on an arm chair with castors. A guitar on the stage.*

STUMP *is discovered in dressing gown, finishing a portrait, R.; CLARA and the two PUPILS are drawing from the lay figure, L. TOM at the back grinding colours on the slab. MRS. STUMP at needlework.*

STUMP. (*goes over to table, L.*) Now, young ladies, how do you get on? Miss Biggs, that is very clever, but I must beg you to observe that both eyes are never seen in a profile. Miss Smith, my love, that ear is large enough for a bonnet. Well, well, you're tired I dare say, I'm sure I am; I won't detain you any longer: good morning, my dears, good morning. Tom, rub out the young ladies. I mean, let out the young ladies. (*goes back to easel*—TOM *shows off the* PUPILS, L., *and re-enters*) Now, Tom, put away the lay figure.
TOM. Come, my beauty, your day's work is over. So move on with your barrow while your wheel's good. (*wheels out lay figure, C. door, and re-enters*)
STUMP. (*goes to portrait*) Now, my lady, when I've starched your collar and brushed your dress a little, you'll do.
CLARA. Finished already, uncle? (*goes up to window at back*)
MRS. S. I should think so by this time. I'm sure he's been so busy the young lady pupils had no lesson this morning at all.
STUMP. Betsy! Mrs. Stump! The needle, my love, is your department, not the pencil. I set my pupils an example of industry, and that alone is worth a guinea a quarter. But what do you think of my picture, eh?
MRS. S. } Oh, charming indeed.
CLARA. }
STUMP. No! do you think so, really. Now, without flattery.
TOM. Well, without flattery, it's devilish good.

An Amateur Playbill of 1853 (*opposite*) and the Play it Advertised

The Acting Edition

Actors and Directors, both amateur and professional, have long had, and still have, their love/hate relationship with our Acting Editions. And quite rightly. At one time designed to give the inexperienced Amateur all the help he could possibly need, even down to where to put his feet, if not his hands, they caused resentment among the more competent who preferred to design their own sets and work out their own production. It was confusing for actors under those conditions to find a set of printed stage directions that conflicted with the Director's plotting, and it was infuriating for the Director to be told by the Actor "But it says I sit here!" On the other hand, our Acting Editions were mighty popular with the weekly Reps who had not the time to work anything out for themselves.

The roots of the Acting Edition are to be found in the early nineteenth-century printed copies which frequently boasted they were "the only edition which is faithfully marked with the Stage Business and Stage Directions as it is performed at the Theatres Royal". The term *Acting Edition* came to be applied to these copies, and the authority of the Prompt Copy established the Definitive Version of the play.

In those early days scenery consisted of backcloths and wings that slid on and off stage in grooves. Windows and doors and non-practical furniture were painted on the canvas, and the actors made their entrances and exits behind the wings. A typical page of one of Lacy's early scripts is reproduced (page 25). Stage business was very much a matter of tradition and actors needed little help other than to have their entrances and exits marked.

It was not until 1841 that the Box Set, complete with ceiling piece, made its first appearance. But it did not immediately replace the older system, which must have represented a vested interest. In 1864 Tom Robertson's *David Garrick* is found using grooves. Robertson, the prototype of Pinero's Tom Wrench, is generally credited with the introduction of the Box Set. With practical doors and windows, and even fireplaces, and real furniture throughout, the Prompt Copy began to record more and more details. By the end of the century the Producer (or Director as we now call him in deference to the Americans) had entered the scene. This new character, soon to be joined by the Designer, had overall responsibility for the interpretation of the author's work, and controlled not only the actors' speaking, but all their movements and handling of props. All this detail was recorded in the Prompt Copy which became a record of The Production.

The Acting Edition was becoming a work that required considerable editorial expertise in its preparation. Sending the Prompt Copy to the printer and hoping for the best would have resulted in considerable chaos. While the author's text was obviously sacrosanct, it was necessary to weigh every stage direction carefully for clarity, and put it in its chronological place. A very careful watch also had to be kept for any conflict in the directions. Prompt scripts were by no means always perfect. Two or even more different sets of directions have been known to be incorporated in the same copy.

The Acting Edition reached its zenith of complication in the second quarter of this century. In *The Ghost Train* (1925) the off-stage Effects required the exertions of fifteen men. The instructions are still printed in our edition of the play for the benefit of those purists who have an aversion to recorded sound and prefer to do their training under sail. In Esther McCracken's play *Quiet Week-End* (1941) the Furniture and Property Plots fill three and a half pages of small print and list over three hundred items.

Until some time in the 1950s the full professional Lighting Plot was also included, regardless of the fact that it referred to a stage that was probably at least four times as large as any that the amateurs were likely to use, and was designed for many times the amount of equipment.

The species was becoming endangered; but it has been saved and is not extinct. Over the last twenty-five years the Acting Edition has adapted to meet the changing styles of writing and stage presentation, and the changing needs of amateur performers, who have become increasingly adventurous and competent. Today, only a skeleton structure of stage directions are included: just sufficient to make sure the action is clear and that anyone following them will not get hopelessly tied up. Some people read plays for pleasure, and they must not find their enjoyment spoiled by unnecessary stage directions that hold up the action for them. On the other hand, the actors must be told what is expected of them, and above all must have the text presented in a manner that is visually conducive to learning their parts—the design and lay-out of the pages is of great importance. Lighting and Effects are now restricted to Cue Plots and a simple description of the effects as the audience is expected to see or hear them. How they are achieved is left to the Director and the Stage Manager.

House Style

Long years ago we took an idle hour and started to codify a very haphazard, untidy and erratic House Style that had grown up rather than been brought up over the previous half century. Evolving a House Style for Acting Editions presents many special problems. How, for example, does one indicate the comings and goings of the various characters to and from the stage? Does one treat *Exit* as a Latin or an English verb? If the former what about *Enter*? They make a balanced pair, but can one be allowed to be in Latin and the other in English? Surely that would be as unthinkable as a mixed metaphor! Does one then funk the issue altogether and use the safer *Comes on* and *Goes off*? But is it safer? The late Agatha Christie wrote a play in which one of the characters was called *Canon Pennefather*. Could one really have the Canon going off? For us *Exit* would have to be an English verb. After all Shakespeare did not write *"They have their Exeunts and their Entrances."*

Once upon a time we employed a free-lance sub-editor who had been brought up in the old school of actors. He would pepper the text of Pantomimes and other comic works with the idiotism (Bus.). It took our Editor, then a new boy and very green in the ways of Old Hams, a long time to realize it was an abbreviation indicating that the actor should introduce some funny business at that point. In vain he requested it should either be omitted or the funny business should be spelt out. But the (Bus.) syndrome was incurable and the Editor had to go through every script himself and delete them all.

French's and the Lord Chamberlain

Enshrined in the Theatres Act 1843 was the law giving the Lord Chamberlain power of life and death over every new play. A copy had to be sent to him a week before its first performance for his licence. This could only be done by the Manager of the Theatre. Neither the Author nor the Publisher could get the licence. For many years French's had to pretend that the first performance of any hitherto unproduced play would take place at the Cripplegate Theatre in the City of London. To substantiate the fiction a member of the staff would be sent there to sit in the centre of the bare stage in the empty theatre and solemnly read the play aloud to himself. Eventually a better working arrangement was established.

Musical Plays

"Operas abroad are plays where every word is sung;
this is not rellished in England."

The Gentleman's Journal, 1693

However, by the end of the nineteenth century the English, and the Americans, had tamed Opera and tempered it to their tastes. They had found that every word did *not* have to be sung, as Offenbach had shown in Paris with his Opera Bouffe, and Strauss in Vienna. In London, W S Gilbert and Arthur Sullivan had formed an unique partnership and had created a new genre, leading the way to the light-hearted frolics of Musical Comedy. In America, this was exemplified by *The Belle of New York*. Three London theatres and one impresario were particularly associated with this form of entertainment: the Adelphi; where Gertie Miller appeared under the management of the Impresario George Edwardes; Daly's, built by Edwardes for the American Manager Augustus Daly; and The Gaiety, also built by Edwardes, and perhaps the best remembered of the lot for its buxom show girls.

Compared to the straight play the Musical was like mountaineering to rock climbing: the scale was magnified ten-fold, or more, and that may have been one reason why French's came late into the field of publishing and handling the amateur rights of them. In addition to the words you needed the music, vocal scores for the singers, and band parts for the orchestra. Altogether a very heavy investment. The first musical to be published by French's was *The Belle of New York* in 1927. This was followed by *La Poupee, The Vagabond King, Rose Marie, Chu Chin Chow, The Desert Song* and *Bitter Sweet*—all at yearly intervals.

Chu Chin Chow had had the distinction of running for 2,238 performances—a record which stood for half-a-century. Its existence, we are told, was owed to a wet week in Manchester. Oscar Asche, the librettist, unable to play golf during a provincial tour, idly decided to write the "Pantomime" he had always intended to compose.

During the 1920s and 1930s "doing a show" usually meant going to a Musical, and many of the classics were produced at this time, later to be added to our list. *Anything Goes, Balalaika, The Dubarry, Magyar Melody, Maritza, No No Nanette, Viktoria and Her Hussar* and *White Horse Inn* all belong to this period.

At this time of the Depression in America people's thoughts had gone back to the land in search of nostalgia and a new confidence, and one of the more successful plays had been Lynn Rigg's *Green Grow the Lilacs*. In the early 1940s French's editor in New York persuaded the Theatre Guild to make a musical of the play. The result was the first of the great musicals that set the style for the whole of the post-war period—*Oklahoma*.

A close relationship was later built up between French's and the librettist Eric Maschwitz and the composers George Ponsford and Bernard Grun, who added, in addition to *Balalaika*, already mentioned, *Goodnight Vienna* and *Waltz Without End*. Later still came *Bless the Bride* from A P Herbert and Vivian Ellis. Following the death of Ivor Novello many of his principal Musicals were acquired, among them *Gay's the Word, Glamorous Night, Perchance to Dream* and *King's Rhapsody* and *The Dancing Years*.

After 1956 it became apparent that some of the earlier Musicals were showing signs of wear. The music was still excellent, but audiences had acquired more sophisticated senses of humour and the comedy had long been outgrown. Eric Maschwitz and others were invaluable in bringing some of these other books up to date and giving the scores a new lease of life.

Since the 1940s there has been a growing demand from amateur Operatic Societies for Musical Plays. The large choruses of the older shows enabled them to use as many of their members as possible (and also to ensure full houses). But they also needed costumes and scenery, and it was here that Charles H Fox and Stage Scenery worked closely with French's to provide the complete service. Fox's could often provide the original costumes, and Stage Scenery the sets that had been used in the West End productions. Unfortunately, many of the theatres used by the Amateur Operatic Societies were smaller than the London ones for which the scenery had been designed, and there were too often acute problems in setting up. The lighting equipment was often inadequate also, and the time available for dress rehearsing in a set that didn't fit was far too short. Considering that the scenery had to be transported the length and breadth of the country in the special waggons used by the railways, together with skip after skip of costumes, the effect was not commensurate with the effort. It was an heroic struggle by the Operatic Societies, and was greatly appreciated by many people, but in the end it proved too cumbersome and expensive. The Societies were compelled to find cheaper ways of producing their shows, and as has happened in the past to follow the lead of the professional theatre: on this occasion by adopting their more austere methods of production.

Today it is usually only the larger amateur societies who can put on the older Musicals, with their heavy demands on chorus, orchestra, and scenery. These shows stay popular because they have a sure recipe for success—good stories accompanied by good scores. But tastes are changing all the time and more and more drama groups are making forays into the musical theatre. For such groups the successes of the 1950s such as *The Boy Friend, Fings Ain't Wot They Used T' Be, Lock Up Your Daughters*, and *Salad Days* have now been joined by more recent, small cast, easy-to-stage, plays such as *Grease, Godspell, Jack the Ripper* and *Something's Afoot*.

Similar considerations apply in America where the market for Musical Plays is of growing importance, and the majority of drama groups stage one every year. Among the current and future releases are *They're Playing Our Song, Chicago, I Love My Wife, Something's Afoot* and *Peter Pan*.

The SCENE Room
at 89 Strand
in 1901

THE SCENE ROOM.
A special paper scenery for amateurs
is one of French's specialities.

29

Our Books—and Other Things
A Complete Service

Throughout the years attempts had been made, by French in Nassau Street and later by the Hoggs, to provide as complete a service as possible to the amateur performer. Lacy had been no exception and during the 1860s he extended his play publishing activities to produce a set of over 400 plates of Dramatic, National and Historical Costumes. They sold for 6d plain and 1s coloured, and tradition has it that an artist was paid one farthing for hand-colouring each plate. How many were issued is not known, but they were still on sale as late as 1946 and some still survive and decorate our bookshop today.

Paper scenery printed in four colours was another service offered by French's. An interior set, in light or dark oak with windows of different sizes, a door and a fireplace and panelled walls were available. Six large sheets of paper went to make up an Oak Tree; and there were various patterns of brick and stonework and fencing; a kitchen fireplace, deal planking, the outside of a house and a whole Proscenium Arch. The paper sheets were intended for mounting on canvas and would transform any large drawing room into a Theatre. The canvas was also on sale—2 yards wide at 1s 6d a yard.

When the business moved to Southampton Street a room in the basement with a specially high ceiling (and still known as the Scenery Room to some older members of the staff!) was used to exhibit the Garden, the Wood, the Drawing-Room and Cottage Scenes; also the Proscenium Paper, Drop Scene and French Window.

The scenery continued to be popular until the late 1940s. Now all that remains are some sheets of Book-Backs that are sufficiently realistic for filling library shelves.

"Brickdust and Hamfat"

Another service once offered by French's was the supply of Theatrical Make-up and, for those who needed it, information on how to use it. In 1877 Samuel French published the first book exclusively on Theatrical Make-Up. The old Pros, their pulses pounding with Traditional Business, needed no books to teach them how to use the crude materials of their trade. If they had not learnt to use them at their mothers' knees they had soon picked up the skill in the hard school of experience. But the Amateurs had no such advantages and needed to be told not only how to apply Make-up but also where to obtain it. French provided the answers, as the pages of his 1884–5 catalogue show.

Concealed behind the anonymity of *Haresfoot & Rouge*, the author of *How to "Make-Up", a Practical Guide*, listed some two dozen materials, including Indian Ink, Burnt Cork, Prepared Whiting, and Powdered Antimony. Also required, if you were to do the job properly, were "Black Crape Masks, Scalps, and some Wool". "Tablettes de Jouvence" were priced at 1s 6d, a "Box of Blue, for Veins" at 3s, and a "Superior Hares Foot" could cost you all of One Shilling. Twenty-three hand-coloured illustrations aided the descriptions of how to use these diabolical ingredients which were best suited to a Witch's Cauldron.

Haresfoot & Rouge was already becoming out of date before the printers' ink had dried. Ten years earlier a German opera singer, Ludwig Leichner, had invented the Grease Paints, though they were slower to cross the Channel than the Atlantic. Even so, the book had a useful life of nearly a quarter of a century before French's put it to bed and brought out a new one by Adair Fitzgerald, a sometime actor who had turned dramatist and journalist. Fitzgerald threw doubt on Herr Leichner's claim to invention by reporting that one Hermann Vezin had told him he had "mixed a lot of colour with melted tallow in Philadelphia in 1857". Whatever the rights and wrongs of this claim and counterclaim, the Grease Paints were a giant step forward, and Fitzgerald's book a smaller step in popularizing them. We don't know what went into the sticks of paint, but powdered antimony was certainly Out, and no-one now needed to die from the effects of whitening his beard. It is interesting to note that many of the same illustrations were used for both these early books: whether this is a clue to the authorship of the first one, or indicative of economy on the part of French we shall probably never know.

After another thirty years Eric Ward's *Book of Make-Up* took the stage. This was probably the most popular book on the subject ever published and would have gone on selling long after it had become hopelessly out of date had French's not withdrawn it. Stage Make-Up had undergone a very considerable change. Developments in cosmetic make-up had not been without their influence. Old materials were discontinued, and new ones were taking their place. TV and Films, Open Stages, Theatre-in-the-Round, and new techniques in Stage Lighting, were all playing their parts in banishing the crude "lines" that had for so long been used by an actor to represent age and character. At the best these "lines" were only effective for a few rows in the mid-stalls. Beyond they were invisible; nearer to they were grotesque.

It took five years to design a successor to Eric Ward's book. The new technique of contouring the face with light and shade, and the new materials, called for a totally new approach, a new type of handbook that could also cope with the changes that would inevitably continue in the supply of the basic material over the next quarter century. In 1977, one hundred years after the first book, the new work by Douglas Young was published under the title *ABC of Stage Make-Up*.

Make-Up continued to be sold at Southampton Street until 1963 when it was passed to Charles H Fox who had better facilities for handling the large range of materials.

Plays and More Plays

And then of course there were the plays themselves. Two important Acts of Parliament, one passed in 1833, the other ten years later, helped to waft the Drama of the nineteenth century out of the doldrums into which it had drifted since the days of Sheridan. The former, often known as Bulwer Lytton's Act, gave the Author the exclusive right to control performances of his own plays—provided they had been published. The obvious need that arose for Authors to get their plays hastily into print can hardly have failed to influence Lacy in his business, and one must wonder whether it was ever his practice to charge for publication. Certainly he seems to have been pretty indiscriminate in his choice and to have preferred quantity rather than quality.

In truth, there wasn't very much quality anyway. The two Patent Theatres, Drury Lane and Covent Garden, had the monopoly of the spoken word, and both were too big for the more intimate and intelligent drama so that they were forced to aim at popular appeal with spectacles and the large-scale effects of Melodrama. The Minor Theatres were limited to plays that spoke to their audiences through Mime and Music mostly. Not until 1843, when the Theatres Act was passed, was the monopoly broken and the Drama freed to develop intelligently. The effect began to show in the 1850s and 1860s with the appearance of such plays as *London Assurance* and *Masks and Faces*, and as the quality of the Drama improved so did the quality of the plays published, and French and Hogg became increasingly selective in the material they sought and accepted. There is a hint that this may have been largely Hogg's influence, and that French left to himself would have been satisfied with quantity.

It is not easy to be precise over the number of plays published by Lacy before he sold out to Samuel French. One can account for something over 1400 up to 1872, but although all his titles were numbered, it was the practice when one went out of print to re-allocate its number to another title. He should have had more consideration for the Theatre Historians of the future. In the 108 years since then more than twice as many plays have been published in Britain alone bringing the total of Lacy and French together to over 4,000.

"Do You Sell Books?"

One fine day in 1967 a woman telephoned and asked "Do you sell books?" Concealing our surprise we assured her we did sell books. We'd been selling books for a very long time. The shop at 89 The Strand, illustrated on page 21, shows how we sold books to a stylish customer in 1901. In those days all the books, or so nearly all as makes no difference, were those published by French's. Everybody interested in plays knew French's and came to buy from us—there was nowhere else to go. When we moved to Southampton Street the showroom was fitted out more as a library than a shop—and so it remains to this day. People came to browse, and some brought their sandwiches and stayed for lunch while selecting plays for performance in the long winter evenings. There were stands with compartments for different categories of plays—Plays arranged according to the numbers of characters; Plays for Children, Plays for Men and Plays for Ladies (a very nice distinction there, and one insisted on by one of the "lady" shop assistants) and Plays for All Occasions. And somewhere not very prominent there were also a few plays that were not controlled by French's, and if anyone had the nerve to ask for one it would reluctantly be produced and exchanged for money.

Recitations, Musical Monologues and Gag Books were also popular and a goodly selection was always to be found together with "Guide Books, Games and Miscellaneous Theatrical Works" including *London Ball-room Guide*, *Dramatic and Musical Law*, *How to Become an Actor* and *Parlour Magic*. Earlier Lacy had been selling *Comic Recitations*, a *Practical Essay on Elocution*, Coulon's *Guide to Fashionable Dancing*, a *History of Punch and Judy* with illustrations by Cruikshank, a number of biographies, and a work with the intriguing title *The Natural History of the Ballet Girl*, by Albert Smith with illustrations by A. Henning.

But by the time our unknown woman telephoned us all that was in the past. The old sliding-doors that separated the window from the shop had gone and passers-by could see inside and know what to expect if they ventured in.

The shelves were now bursting with books from all over England and America, and which outnumbered French's own publications by more than five to one. The "library" atmosphere was carried through by a unique indexing system which to the present day aims to reference all publications about the theatre and related arts, whether or not they are stocked by the bookshop.

The old recitation books had been replaced by more up-to-date publications to aid the amateur, and professional, performer. Books of poems and prose for elocution work, make-up cards, an anthology of tongue-twisters, monologue and duologue books, a comedian's handbook and a guidebook for the performance of Shakespeare's plays are among the latest additions.

The shop had become The Theatre Bookshop, specializing in plays and books on the Theatre, backed with unique knowledge and experience on both sides of the Atlantic.

Choosing the Right Play

The vast increase in the number of plays available for performance and the influx of American drama has made the *Guide to Selecting Plays* even more valuable than when Wentworth Hogg first published it. Today's *Guide* has undergone a number of changes. There has been considerable re-arrangement and cross referencing, but the most notable change has been in the descriptions of the characters in the plays. When it was first published the characters were described in terms of the actors and actresses in a Stock Company who would be called upon to play them. The Tragedian, the Juvenile Lead, the Light Comedian and the Low Comedian were all clearly recognizable and plays were written with parts for them. So too were the Leading Lady; the Ingénue, the Heavy Lead (who played the Villians of Melodrama) and the Heavy Woman (who played Lady Macbeth). But from early on in this century authors were gradually demolishing this family. The Tragedian was one of the first to go—plays were not being written for him. By the 1950s styles in acting had become more subtle and actors were being called upon to produce characters that often transcended several of the old classifications in one part, and it became essential to describe the part and not the player. The fact that the *Guide* had not been brought up to date for ten years owing to the War provided the opportunity, when it was reprinted in 1950, to make this very necessary change.

The equivalent publication in America, known more simply as *French's Basic Catalogue of Plays*, goes out to 65,000 people and runs to some 400 pages. Nineteen Pulitzer Prize winners are included among the plays it lists.

The Price of Perfection

"Send thirteen postage-stamps to Mr. Samuel French, of the Strand, and you will receive back 'The Guide to Selecting Plays, or Manager's Companion,' which will give you the whole information you request in a nutshell."

"DEAR MR. S.,—Our young people are thinking of getting up some private theatricals at no distant date, and all the arrangements are made. But we are in some considerable doubt about the selection of a suitable play. Each one has a different opinion on the matter, but the girls beg me to ask you to decide for them. You really know so very much more about plays than we do, that I am sure you will kindly spare a moment out of your valuable time and help us out of our dilemma. We can count upon a company of half-a-dozen. A youth and a maiden fairly good, the rest with scant experience.—Yours faithfully, L. M. A."

Clement Scott. Editor of *The Theatre* & Dramatic Critic of the *Daily Telegraph*

Birmingham Daily Gazette
Friday, November 25, 1881.
[BY E. L. BLANCHARD.]
Thursday Night.

With long winter evenings to be provided for, and social gatherings in country houses to be entertained, the topic of "amateur theatricals" now becomes a frequent subject of discussion over the family fireside. As a general rule complete ignorance prevails as to the most suitable pieces for selection, and when the choice is eventually made the manner in which the characters should be impersonated becomes a problem most difficult of solution. Generally a professional actor is invited to come down and superintend the arrangements, or a confident friend whose knowledge of theatrical matters is supposed to be extensive is pressed into the service, and asked to afford them the benefit of whatever information he may have acquired in a desultory way through an occasional gossip with actors at their clubs. For weeks before the great event comes off letters are written to the editors of theatrical newspapers and those presumed to be learned in the mysteries of the stage to know the proper dresses to wear, the right colours to choose, and the peculiar mode of marking the face so as to enable a stripling to assume the aspect of senility, or impart to the aspiring tragedian of the domestic circle the complexion of a swarthy Moor.

Sounds Effective

A recent innovation in the Theatre Bookshop has been the creation of a collection of recorded Sound Effects. The Fifteen Shades gliding silently about in the previously mentioned *Ghost Train* are no longer needed. They have been superseded by one Stage Person sitting in comfort somewhere behind the audience coldly pressing buttons with clinical detachment. The resulting sounds may be more predictable and identical from performance to performance, but for every gain there must be a loss, and the excitement and exhilaration of "getting it right on the night" have gone for good for those fifteen men. But however much we may deplore the loss of fun in having to work wind and rain machines, and thunder sheets, and explosion tanks, and horses printing their proud coco-nuts on the unyielding boards, we have to keep up with technology. There is no longer any need to exercise your skill and ingenuity devising the sound of an Avalanche or a Spanish Bullfight, neither of which you have probably ever attended, or to argue about the pitch of a Natterjack Toad's croak. We have spent the last few years amassing a Catalogue of hundreds of world-wide Sound Effects on English, French, German and American discs and tapes, and it needs no imagination whatsoever to come to us and buy the Real Thing on a shiny black record.

Where Next?

Gazing into crystal baubles is notoriously misleading and unproductive. But on past performance we should be able to hazard a guess that the Amateur Theatre will continue to flourish and refuse to be discouraged by having to work in impossible conditions.

Among Englishmen there are those who like taking off most of their clothes and playing violent games to get warm again. They call it Sport. This has long been encouraged because it is considered "healthy". *Mens sana in corpore sano*. Maybe it produces the *corpore sano* but often there is no *mens* at all. On the other hand Cultural activities, which produce plenty of *mens* without worrying about the *corpore*, if not regarded as being positively degenerate, have been looked upon as private amusement undeserving of any public support. We are talking of course of the Amateur world, not the professional . . .

But now there are signs that this attitude is changing; though some people still exist who take the view "they only do it to satisfy their own egos; and anyway who wants to endure the agony of watching an amateur show?"

Slowly it would seem the Amateur Theatre is beginning to find its place in the Community. In parts of the country it is often the only theatre there is; but in the larger towns, where there is a professional Entertainment Industry, it has to decide whether it will compete or complement.

In Britain the Amateur Theatre is fighting to be recognized as much a Recreational necessity as Sport and Swimming, and to take its place among Night Classes and Public Libraries. It will only succeed if it achieves high standards and gives good value. French's job is to see that the raw materials are to hand, and the technical information on how to get the best out of them.

In America the dramatic expansion and development of the United States has been matched by the growth of French's, which in 150 years has survived the Civil War, two World Wars and the great Depression, and continues to be untiring in its search for the world's best plays.

That there should be differences of emphasis in the development of French's in London and New York is inevitable. Social and intellectual differences, different legal systems and copyright laws, different theatrical and commercial practices, have all had their influences; but still these two specialist businesses have remained remarkably similar, and have continued to complement and supplement each other.

Lacy laid a sound foundation, French brought from America his useful commercialism, the Hoggs added the confidence that springs from a very high degree of integrity. But no Company can thrive only on its leading actors, and French's has been fortunate in having a supporting cast whose commitment and involvement has been second to none.

Authors of Plays and Books in our Current List

A

Marta Abba
George Abbott
Lionel Abel
Marcel Achard
Robert Allan Ackerman
Rodney Ackland
Lee Adams
George Ade
Ella Adkins
James Agee
Howard Agg
Charles Aidman
George L Aiken
Jean Aiken
Angela Ainley-Jeans
Chingiz Aitmatov
Zoe Akins
Edward Albee
Ronald Alexander
William Alfred
James Allardice
Frank Allen
Janet Allen
Jay Presson Allen
Ralph P Allen
Woody Allen
John Allison
John Anderson
Leroy Anderson
Maxwell Anderson
Robert Anderson
Charlton Andrews
Leonid Andreyev
Morris Ankrum
Jean Anouilh
Rock Anthony
Robert L Antrim
John Antrobus
Don Appell
Ray Aranha
William Archer
William Archibald
Jane Arden
John Arden
Reginald Arkell
Anthony Armstrong
Charl Armstrong
Larry Arrick
Alvin Aronson
Fernando Arrabal
William Arrowsmith
Oscar Asche
Herbert Ashton
Leopold Atlas
George Alexrod
Alan Ayckbourn
Juliet Aykroyd
Marcel Ayme
Ethan Ayer

B

Thomas Babe
Frank Bacon
Enid Bagnold
William Baines
Edna Baker
John L Balderston
James Baldwin
Frank Ballard
Frances Banks
Lynne Reid Banks
Kay Bannerman
Frank Barasch
Richard R Barbie
Pierre Barillet
Albert Barker
Edwin L Barker
Howard McKent Barnes
John Barker
Peter Barnes
Wilson Barnes
Alec Baron
James Lee Barrett
J M Barrie
Bob Barry
Philip Barry
William Edwin Barry
Stan Barstow
Jean Bart
Lionel Bart
John Barton
Jacques Barzun
Sam Bate
George Batson
E Dora Battison
A & G Baumrucker
Clifford Bax
Lewis Beach
Samuel Beckett
Henry Becque
Brendan Behan
S N Behrman
Albert Bein
David Belasco
Ben Belitt
Gordon Bell
Mary Hayley Bell
Geoffrey Bellman
Saul Bellow
Derek Benfield
Alan Bennett
Dorothy Bennett
John Bennett
Michael Bennett
Benrimo
Sally Benson
Josephine Bentham
Eric Bentley
Herbert Berghof
Alan Bergman
Marilyn Bergman
Reginald Berkeley

Ralph Berkey
Julie Berna
William Beney
Elmer Bernstein
Daniel Berrigan
Rudolph Besier
Rick Besoyan
Ugo Betti
Richard Beynon
Richard Bimonte
Kenneth Bird
Helen Gary Bishop
John Bishop
Angela Black
Franklyn Black
Ian Stuart Black
Kitty Black
Vera Blackwell
Iain Blair
Simpson Bland
Ralph Blane
Dorothy Blankfort
Michael Blankfort
Jerry Blatt
Lee Blessing
Bertram Bloch
Ursula Bloom
Robert Bloomfield
Dan Blue
Maureen Blythe
Richard Blythe
Sam Bobrick
Jerry Bock
David Boehm
John Boland
Joseph Bologna
Robert Bolt
Carl Eugene Bolte
Barbara Bolton
Guy Bolton
C G Bond
Edward Bond
Nelson Bond
Leslie Bonnett
Anthony Booth
John Hunter Booth
Jill Booty
Alan Boretz
James Borrelli
John Boruff
Dion Boucicault
William Boswell
Julie Bovasso
John Bowen
Terence Bowen
Paul Bowles
Derek Bowskill
Muriel Box
Sidney Box
Mary Boylan
Parnell Bradbury
Benjamin Bradford

Alfred Bradley
M Bradley-Dyne
Leo Brady
Forbes Bramble
Mark Bramble
Dorothy Brandon
Bertolt Brecht
E C Brereton
Romney Brent
Lowell Brentano
Harvey Brett
Michael Brett
Neville Brian
James Bridie
Mary Elizabeth Briggs
Harold Brighouse
John M. Brinnin
Stephen Bristol
Robert Brittan
K P Britton
Jay Broad
George Broadhurst
James Brock
Eric Brogger
Harold Brooke
Cyrus Brooks
Jeremy Brooks
Kenneth Brown
Lew Brown
Nathan Brown
Steve Brown
William F Brown
E Martin Browne
Felicity Browne
Maurice Browne
Porter Emerson Browne
Wynyard Browne
John C Brownell
Renaud C Bruce
Neville J Bryant
Thomas Brynes
Mabel Buchanan
Art Buchwald
Mark Bucci
George Buchner
Anthony Buckeridge
Sheila Buckley
Ed Bullins
Michael Bullock
Stuart Burge
Edwin Burke
Johnny Burke
Stewart Burke
Barbara Burnham
Anne Burr
Abe Burrows
John Burrows
Lonnie Burstein
Wendell Burton
David Butler
Ivan Butler

C

Sammy Cahn
Erskine Caldwell
T J Camp
François Campaux
Lawton Campbell
Norman Campbell
Roy Campbell
David Campton
Albert Camus
Denis Cannan
Alice M Cannon
Karel Capek
Jeannette Carlisle
Fred Carmichael
Al Carmines
Frank Carney
Joseph Carole
Leon Carr
Jean Claude Carrière
John Carroll
Paul Vincent Carroll
Arthur Carter
Beatrix Carter
Horace E Carter
Margaret Carter
Randolph Carter
Falkland L Cary
Rosemary Casey
Warren Casey
Vera Caspary
Alberto Cassella
Mary Lou Cassidy
Harry Cauley
David Caute
Henry Cecil
Miguel de Cervantes
Alice Chadwicke
John Chapman
Eric Chappell
Erik Charell
Mark Charlap
Moie Charles
Olive Chase
Paddy Chayefsky
Syd Cheatle
Anton Chekhov
Gwen Cherrel
Paul Cherry
Alice Childress
Edward Chodorov
Jerome Chodorov
Richard B Chodosh
Agatha Christie
Campbell Christie
Dorothy Christie
Jay Christopher
Donald Churchill
Ross Clairborne
Brian Clark
Gwyn Clark
Ron Clark

35

David Clarke
Stanley Clayton
Brian Clemens
Le Roy Clemens
Samuel Clemens
Colin Clements
John Clements
P M Clepper
John Clifton
Joel Climenhaga
Edward Clinton
V C Clinton-Baddeley
David Climie
Harry Clork
D L Coburn
Ronald Cockram
Jean Cocteau
Lenore Coffee
Denise Coffey
George M Cohan
Peter Coke
Tom Cole
Cy Coleman
Thomas Coley
Constance Collier
Lester Colodny
John Colton
Betty Comden
Anne Commire
Howard Comstock
E P Conkle
Louise Conkling
Joe Connelly
Mare Connelly
Barry Connors
Denis Constanduros
Mabel Constanduros
G R Cook
Peter Cook
Ray Cooney
Jacques Copeau
David Copelin
Alec Coppel
Norman Corwin
W Ernest-Cossons
James Costigan
Noël Coward
William Joyce Cowen
Constance Cox
J J Coyle
Paul Crabtree
Lor Crane
Frank Craven
Eskel Crawford
M Creagh-Henry
Luigi Creatore
Tom Cregan
Michael Cristofer
Jordan Crittenden
Fernand Crommelynck
Beverley Cross
Rachel Crothers

Jean Croue
Russel Crouse
Mart Crowley
Thomas Cruden
Floyd Crutchfield
Gretchen Cryer
Alan Cullen
Derek Cunningham
Louis L Curcio
Jane Curtin
Catherine C Cushing
Neil Cuthbert
Adam Czerniawski

D

Louis D'Alton
Robert Dahdah
Adrian Dale
Jim Dale
Augustin Daly
William Dalzell
Margaretta D'Arcy
James Damico
Clemence Dane
Guy Daniels
Leslie Darbon
Gwen Davenport
Frederick Davies
Harry Davies
Gordon Daviot
Dorrance Davis
Flanagan Davis
Ossie Davis
Owen Davis
Doris M Day
Holman Day
Hamilton Deane
Harris Deans
Terence Deary
A H Debenham
Peter Dee
Sylvia Dee
Eduardo de Fillipo
Denis de Marne
Emile de Najac
R F Delderfield
Harry Delf
Jeffrey Dell
Vina Delmar
Louis del Grande
Reginald Denham
Henry Denker
Richard Dennis
Norman Denny
Joyce Dennys
Edward Dept
Daphne Derrick
B G DeSylva
Maurice Desvalliere
Jacques Deval
Peter Devries
James Paul Dey

C Stafford Dickens
John Dighton
Alan Dinehart
Michael Dines
William Dinner
Dorothy Dinroe
Beulah Dix
John F Donaldson
Harriet Donleavy
Thomas Doran
Nat Dorfman
Felicity Douglas
Jeanette Dowling
Arthur Conan Doyle
Monte Doyle
Mary Drayton
Theodore Dreiser
John Drinkwater
Allen Drury
Carolyn Drury
Daphne du Maurier
Costa du Reis
Martin Duberman
Matt Dubey
Edward Dudowicz
Vincent Duffy
Friedrich Durrenmatt
Ashley Dukes
Janet Dunbar
Ronald Duncan
Frank Dunlop
Richard Dunlop
Mary Dunn
Philip Dunning
Lord Dunsany
Christopher Durang
Francis Durbridge
C S Durer
Delray K Dvoracek
Teresa Dzieduszycka
Charles Dyer

E

Edward Eager
George Eastman
Ken Easton
Fred Ebb
Mignon Eberhart
Maurice Edelman
David Edgar
Lee Edwards
Abe Einhorn
Lon Elder
Dennis Eliot
T S Eliot
Irving Elman
Kenneth Elmslie
Donald Elser
Edward Elsey
Charles Emery
Robert Emmett
Barry England

Henry Ephron
Phoebe Ephron
Julius J Epstein
Chester Erskin
Dale Eunson
Dorothy Evans
E Eynon Evans
Will Evans
Joanna Evers
Tom Eyen
Ronald Eyre

F

Diego Fabbri
I B Fagan
Seamus Fail
William Fairchild
Thomas F Fallon
Zina Fallon
Eleanor Farjeon
Herbert Farjeon
William Faulkner
Terence Feely
Jules Feiffer
Ed Feilbert
Gene Feist
Malcolm Fellows
Edna Ferber
J A Ferguson
Walter Ferris
Ted Fetter
John Ferzacca
Georges Feydeau
Salisbury Field
Dorothy Fields
Joseph Fields
Robert Finch
Robert Fisher
Steve Fisher
Clyde Fitch
F Scott Fitzgerald
Rolf Fjelde
Michael Flanders
Martin Flavin
Lucille Fletcher
Peter Florin
John Floyd
Louis Flynn
Paul Finney
A Fodor
Ladislas Fodor
Henry D G Foord
Alistair Foot
Marion de Forest
Joan Ford
Nancy Ford
Ruth Ford
Maria Irene Forres
E M Forster
Anthony Forsythe
Giovacchino Forzano
Kenelm Foss

Bob Fosse
Paul Foster
Rosemary Foster
E M Fotheringham
Terry Curtis Fox
J O Francis
Sister Mary Francis
William Francis
Dimitri Frenkel Frank
Larry Frank
Caroline Franke
Rose Franken
J E Franklin
Jessica Fraser
Mario Fratti
Michael Frayn
Bernard Frechtman
Donald Freed
Dave Freeman
David Freeman
David E Freeman
Stan Freeman
Bob Fremont
David French
Herbert S French
Florida Friebus
William Friedberg
Bruce Jay Friedman
Gary William Friedman
Brian Friel
Rudolph Friml
Ketti Frings
Terence Frisby
Rex Frost
Gerald Frow
Athol Fugard
Albert C Fuller
Dean Fuller
Douglas Furber
George Furth

G

Lewis Galantiere
John Galsworthy
W Randolph Galvin
John Gardiner
Herb Gardner
Ira Gassmann
Dilys Gater
Eleanor Gates
Tudor Gates
Helen Gaubert
Bill Gavin
Noel Gay
Charles Gaynor
Michael Gazzo
Larry Gelbart
Gary Geld
John Gemmell
Pam Gems
Jean Genet
Peter A Gent

Charles George
Robert Gerlach
Dan Gerould
Eleanor Gerould
Leonard Gershe
George Gershwin
Ira Gershwin
Clark Gesner
Steven Gethers
Will Ghelman
Margaret Gibbs
Sheridan Gibney
William Gibson
André Gide
James Gidney
Marnix Gijsen
Michael Gilbert
Willie Gilbert
Peter Gill
William Gillette
Sidney Gilliat
Frank Gilroy
Jean Giltene
Abram Ginnes
Norman Ginsbury
Paul Giovanni
Jean Giradoux
Peter Glenville
Montague Glass
James Gleason
Al Glew
William Glickman
Augustus Goetz
Ruth Goetz
Frances Goforth
Don Goggin
Harry Golden
Bill Goldenberg
Miriam Goldina
James Goldman
Robert Goldman
Angel Goldsby
Robert Goldsby
Lena Goldschmidt
Oliver Goldsmith
Gloria Gonzalez
William Goodhart
Arthur Goodman
Jules Eckert Goodman
Randolph Goodman
Frances Goodrich
Louis Goodrich
Ernest Goodwin
Kurtz Gordon
Richard Gordon
Ruth Gordon
Steve Gordon
Charles Gordone
Christopher Gore
Mordecai Gorelik
Carlos Gorostiza
Bernard Goss

Ivan Gott
Alex Gottlieb
Heywood Gould
James Gow
Ronald Gow
Richard M Grace
Ed Graczk
Barry Grael
John Graham
Mona Graham
Alec Grahame
Ron Grainer
Fred Grandy
Suzanne Granfield
Bob Grant
Micki Grant
Wilfred Grantham
Grattan
Jack Gray
Simon Gray
Jean Gredy
Adolph Green
Carolyn Green
Mawby Green
Paul Green
Michael Green
Graham Greene
Patterson Greene
Mary Greenslade
Duncan Greenwood
Walter Greenwood
Lady Gregory
Joyce Grenfell
Jeffrey Grenfell-Hill
Joe Edward Grenzeback
William Grew
Edward Grieg
Susan Griffin
Krystyna Griffith-Jones
Trevor Griffiths
John Grimsey
Milton Gropper
Larry Grossman
Suzanne Grossman
John Guare
Gerardo Guerrieri
Arthur Guiterman
A R Gurney
Alexander Guyan
Clara Gyorgyey

H

Hal Hackady
Albert Hackett
Walter Hackett
Ronald Hadlington
James Hagan
Albert Hague
George Haight
George Haimsohn
Nathan Hale
Ruth Hale

Bob Hall
Nick Hall
Willis Hall
David Halliwell
Nancy Hamilton
Patrick Hamilton
Marvin Hamlisch
Christopher Hampton
Ronald Hanmer
Link Hannah
Lorraine Hansbery
Shirley Hansen
Otto Harbach
Huntly Harding
John Harding
Margaret Harding
M Hardwick
David Hare
Roy Hargrave
Sheldon Harnick
Jack Harrigan
Aurand Harris
Elmer Harris
John Harris
Lionel Harris
Richard Harris
Vernon Harris
Donald Harron
Elizabeth Hart
Moss Hart
Stan Hart
Stanley Hart
Brett Harte
Anne Harvey
Frank Harvey
Wilfred Harvey
Christopher Hassall
Charlotte Hastings
Hugh Hastings
F Hatton
George Hauger
William Hauptman
Robin Hawdon
Jim Hawkins
Ruth Hawthorne
Charles Hawtrey
Ian Hay
Alfred Hayes
Joseph Hayes
John E Hazard
George Hazelton
Ben Hecht
Ed Heghinian
Jack Heifner
Herman Heijermans
Joseph Heller
Lilian Hellman
Arnold Helsby
Tony Hendra
A P Herbert
John Herbert
Victor Herbert

James Leo Herlihy
George Herman
Jerry Herman
James Herne
John Hersey
J Hesketh
John D Hess
Dorothy Heyward
Pentland Hick
Derek Hickman
Robert Higgins
Kay Hill
Ken Hill
Lucienne Hill
Robert Hill
Robert J Hilliard
Barry L Hillman
Roger O Hirson
Peter Hoar
Fritz Hochwaelder
Cary Hoffmann
Derek Hoddinott
Horace Hodges
Norman Holland
Anslem Hollo
Daniel Hollywood
Marjorie Holmes
Lawrence Holofcener
Maurice Holstock
Will Holt
William Douglas Home
Edward Honig
Nina Warner Hooke
Brian Hooker
Arthur Hopkins
John Hopkins
Pauline Hopkins
Avery Hopwood
Israel Horovitz
Kenneth Horne
Peter Horsler
Arnold Horwitt
A E Hotchner
Stanley Houghton
Ron House
F Morton Howard
Leslie Howard
Sydney Howard
Donald Howarth
Tina Howe
Cheng-Chin Hsiung
S I Hsiung
Hatcher Hughes
Cyril Hume
Kitty Hunter-Blair
Harold Hutchinson
Aldous Huxley
John Hyman
John B Hymer
Audrey Hyslop

I

Henrik Ibsen
William Inge
Eugene Ionesco
Louis Iribarne
Frederick Isham
Alexandra Ivanoff

J

Douglas Jackson
Frederick Jackson
Nagle Jackson
Jim Jacobs
Michael Jacobs
W W Jacobs
Kenneth Jacobson
Henry James
Carl Jampel
Martin Jarvis
Ronald Jeans
Robinson Jeffers
Charles A Jeffrey
Stephen Jeffreys
Ray Jenkins
Gertrude Jennings
Helen Jerome
Jerome K Jerome
Thomas Job
Errol John
Miriam John
Glyn Johnson
Gregory Johnson
Karen Johnson
Laurie Johnson
Mike Johnson
Nunally Johnson
Pamela Johnson
Philip Johnson
Richard T Johnson
Denis Johnston
Frank Jones
Glyn Jones
Graham Jones
Gwenyth Jones
Helena Jones
Leroy Jones
Paul Jones
Peter Jones
Eric Jones-Evans
Kenneth Jupp

K

Erich Kaestner
Franz Kafka
Judy Kahan
Pavel Kahout
Lucille Kallen
John Kander
Fay Kanin
Garson Kanin
Michael Kanin
Leonard Kantor
Roger Karshner

Jerome Kass
Rose Kastner
Leon Katz
Esther Kaufman
George Kaufman
Mildred Kayden
Benjamin Kay
Valentine Kaytayev
Barrie Keeffe
John Donald Kelly
Anthony Paul Kelly
George Kelly
Tim Kelly
Adrienne Kennedy
Aubrey Kennedy
Charles Kennedy
Jimmy Kennedy
Mary Kennedy
Walter Kent
Allan Kenward
Jean Kerr
John Kerr
Sophie Kerr
Leo Kerz
Ken Kesey
Lyle Kessler
Paul Kester
Michael Kilgarriff
Jerome Kilty
Bruce Kimes
Anthony Kimmins
Philip King
Robert King
Rufus King
Stephen King-Hall
Sidney Kingsley
Jeremy Kingston
Ernest Kinoy
Heinar Kipphardt
Jack Kirkland
John Kirkpatrick
James Kirkwood
Charles Klein
Warren Kliewer
Woody Kling
Frederick Kohner
Frederick Knott
Arthur Kopit
Norma Krasna
Helen Kromer
Louis Kronenberger
Clare Kummer
John B Kuntz
David Kurani
Harry Kurnitz

L

Eugene Labiche
Kevin Laffan
Millard Lampell
Evla A Lamphere
Lee Langley

Noël Langley
Lawrence Langner
Jean Lee Latham
Charles Laughton
Frank Launder
Charles Laurence
Dan Laurence
Arthur Laurents
Emmet Lavery
Warner Law
Ray Lawler
Jerome Laurence
James Lee
Lance Lee
Leslie Lee
Maureen Lee
Robert E Lee
John Leeming
Franz Lehar
Carolyn Leigh
Mike Leigh
Gilbert Lennox
Hugh Leonard
Eugenie Leontovich
Warner Le Roy
Alain-Rene Lesage
Anthony Lesser
Elliott Lester
Francis Letton
Philip Levene
Stephen Levi
Ira Levin
Benn W Levy
Richard Lewine
Ira Lewis
Morgan Lewis
Don Lind
Howard Lindsay
Arthur Livingston
Arthur Sumner Long
Paul Loomis
Anita Loos
Federico Garcia Lorca
Robert Lorick
Arthur Lovegrove
Robert Lowell
Jean Bernard Luc
Claire Boothe Luce
William Luce
Laurence Luckinbill
Peter Luke
Barre Lyndon
Marjorie Lyon
Eugene Lyons

M

James Mabbe
Edward Mabley
Charles MacArthur
Pauline Macaulay
Galt McDermot
Robert D MacDonald

Norman Macdonald
Roger MacDougall
Bill McIlwraith
Helen MacInnes
Gayer Mackey
Philip Mackie
Archibald MacLeish
Margaret Macnamara
Arthur Macrae
Harry Madden
Maurice Maeterlink
Wes Magee
Claude Magnier
Richard Maibaum
Charles Malamuth
Patricia Malango
Nevil Malin
Stephen Mallatratt
Miles Malleson
David Mamet
Charles Mander
Joe Manchester
Frank Mandel
Julie Mandel
Loring Mandel
Mel Mandel
Ralph Manheim
Bill Manhoff
Bettine Manktelow
J Hartley Manners
Albert Mannheiner
Robert Marasco
Felicien Marceau
Max Marcin
Lynda Marchal
Frank Marcus
Walter Marks
Anthony Marriott
Edward Owen Marsh
Armina Marshall
Allan Langdon Martin
Bernice Martin
Edouard Martin
Gilbert Martin
Hugh Martin
Norman Martin
Joyce F Martins
Mel Marvin
Arthur Marx
Eric Maschwitz
Valerie Maskell
A E W Mason
Judie Mason
Rosemary Mason
Wilfred Massey
Joe Masteroff
Lilian Masters
Robert Masters
Robin Maugham
Somerset Maugham
Marcelle Maurette
François Mauriac

Ronald Mavor
Frederick May
Vladimir Mayakovsky
Edwin Mayer
Paul A Mayer
Margaret Mayo
Beatrice Mayor
E Clayton McCarthy
William McCleery
Esther McCracken
Bill McCreary
R Gordon McCullun
Carson McCullers
James McDonald
Robert McEnroe
Elizabeth Apthorp McFadden
W A McGuire
Charles McIntosh
Norman McKinnel
Gene McKinney
Maurice McLoughlin
P J McLoughlin
Terence McNally
Patterson McNutt
Bernard J McOwen
Russell Medcraft
Joseph Mellish
Daniel Meltzer
Alan Melville
Herman Melville
Glen Melvyn
David Mercer
William Merchant
Roy Cooper Mergrue
Bob Mervill
Eve Merriam
Henriette Metcalf
Peter Meyer
Sidney Michaels
Marc Michel
Bernard Miles
Carlton Miles
Ronald Millar
Alice Miller
Helen Miller
Jason Miller
Jonathan Miller
Robin Miller
Clifford Mills
Hugh Mills
A A Milne
Roger Milner
Ron Milner
Robert Milton
Lee Minhoff
Julian Mitchell
Norma Mitchell
Ronald Elwy Mitchell
Newt Mitzman
Molière
Tirso de Molina
Elick Moll

Ferenc Molnar
James Montgomery
Robert Montgomery
Patricia Montley
Carlyle Moore
Carroll Moore
Dudley Moore
Edward J Moore
Nancy Moore
Al Morgan
Charles Morgan
Diana Morgan
Elaine Morgan
Al Moritz
Albert Moritz
Robert Morley
Katherine Morrill
Aldyth Morris
Lloyd Morris
T B Morris
Anne Morrison
Fred Morrit
John Mortimer
Hugh Morton
William Morum
Tad Mosel
Arnold Moss
Cedric Mount
Anna Cora Mowat
Patricia Moyes
Lance Mulcahy
Hans Muller
Robert S Mulligan
Helen Murdoch
Iris Murdoch
Ralph Murphy
John Murray
Thomas Murray
William Murray
Thomas Muschamp
Alfred de Musset
Peter Myers

N

Emile de Najac
Susan Nanus
Leah Napolin
Richard N Nash
Ogden Nash
Paul Nathan
Bill Naughton
Jack Nelson
Robert Nemiroff
Pablo Neruda
John Neville-Andrews
Peter R Newman
Maureen Nield
Ann Nichols
Peter Nichols
Robert Nichols
Kenyon Nicholson
Ariadne Nicolaeff

Authors of Plays and Books in Our Current List (cont)

osephina Niggli
William Noble
Charles Nolte
ohn Ford Noonan
William Norfolk
Frank Norman
Clyde North
Pat Norris
vor Novello
Elliott Nugent
C Nugent
N Richard Nusbaum

O

André Obey
Arch Oboler
ustin O'Brien
iam O'Brien
ean O'Casey
Richard O'Connell
Clifford Odets
ohn O'Donnell
Geoffrey O'Hara
Kevin O'Morrison
Charles O'Neal
ugene O'Neill
Russell O'Neill
Byron Ongley
George Oppenheimer
Robert Ord
tvan Orkeny
oe Orton
George Orwell
aul Osborn
ohn Osborne
ustin O'Toole
ulton Oursler
lun Owen
rmitage Owen
ill Owen
ochelle Owens

P

ric Paice
William Packard
ann Page
el Pahl
ing Palmer
Winifred Palmer
George Panetta
dward Paramore
nil Park
avid Parker
orothy Parker
ouglas Parker
en Parker
ouis N Parker
ewart Parker
erek Parkes
ouglas Parkhirst
en Parkin
onald Parr

John Dos Passos
John Patrick
Robert Patrick
Frances G Patton
H M Paull
Glenn Payton
Herbert Payne
L du Garde Peach
Alan Peacock
V A Pearn
Haakon Pederbach
Ron Pember
Brock Pemberton
S G Perelman
Edward Percy
Hugo Peretti
Issac Loeb Peretz
Eleanor Perry
Jack Perry
Guy Pertwee
Michael Pertwee
Roland Pertwee
Diane Peters
Louis Peterson
David Pethybridge
Pauline Phelps
Winifred Phelps
Eden Philpotts
John Pickard
June Pierson
Arthur W Pinero
Miguel Pinero
Harold Pinter
Don Pippen
Luigi Pirandello
George Pitts
Alan Plater
Stephen Poliakoff
Channing Pollock
Bernard Pomerance
Alan Poole
Pamela Pope
Jack Popplewell
H T Porter
W H Post
Dennis Potter
William Pratt
Peter Preston
Stanley Price
J B Priestley
David Procktor
Nancy Protter
Derek Prouse
Frank Provo
Jack Pulman
John W Pulver
Reginald Purdell
Richard Purdy
John Purves

Q

Serafin Quintero

R

David Rabe
Derek Raby
Thom Racina
Henzie Raeburn
John Ramsay
Bob Randall
Marjorie Randle
Clemence Randolph
John R Raphael
Samuel Raphaelson
Frederick Rath
Terence Rattigan
Santha Rama Rau
Herman Raucher
John Ravold
Joyce Rayburn
David Rayfiel
James Reach
Stuart Ready
Dennis Reardon
Michael Redgrave
Harold Rednour
Skip Redwine
Mark Reed
Theodore Reeves
Sylvia Regan
John Reich
Dave Reieser
Carl Reiner
Max Reitmann
Costa du Rels
Dorothy Reynolds
J B Reynolds
Tim Reynolds
Ronald Ribman
Elmer Rice
Kathleen Rich
Anna S Richardson
Claibe Richardson
Howard Richardson
Robert Riche
David Richmond
John Richmond
Arnold Ridley
J P Riewerts
Lynn Riggs
Lawrence Riley
Mary Roberts Rinehart
David Rintels
Norman Robbins
Ben Roberts
Don Roberts
Rhoda Roberts
Walter Charles Roberts
Lanie Robertson
W Grahame Robertson
David Robinson
Fred Robinson
Lennox Robinson
Noël Robinson
John Roc

Charles Rock
Mary Rodgers
William Roerick
Jack Roffey
David Rogers
Fernando de Rojas
Michael Roloff
Jules Romains
Lawrence Roman
Sigmund Romberg
Ann Ronell
Audrey Roos
William Roos
Lynn Root
L Arthur Rose
Edward Rose
Philip Rose
Reginald Rose
James Rosenberg
Milton Rosenstock
Andrew Rosenthal
George Ross
Judith Ross
Stella Ross
Austin Rosser
Philip Roth
Jerome Rothenberg
Fritz Rotter
André Roussin
Aurania Rouverol
David E Rowley
Tadeusz Rozewicz
Daniel Rubin
Theodore Issac Rubin
H F Rubinstein
Enid Rudd
David Rudkin
Sheila Ruskin
Charles L Russell
Roy Russell
Willy Russell
Miriam Ryan
Florence Ryerson
Morrie Ryskind
Royce Ryton

S

Andrew Sachs
Norman Sachs
Howard Sackler
Carol Bayer Sager
K O Samuel
Mark Sandrich
Alvan Sapinsley
Victorien Sardou
William Saroyan
Emilie Sarter
Jean Paul Sartre
Stan Satlin
Bob Satuloff
James Saunders
Lilian Saunders

Tupper Saussy
Alfred Savoir
Gerald Savory
Michael Sawyer
Ray Scantlin
Milton Schafer
Neil Schaffner
George Schlatter
Robert Schlitt
Walter Schneir
John Scholes
Joseph Schrank
Budd Schulberg
Arnold Schulman
Lawrence Schwab
Lloyd J Schwartz
Stephen Schwartz
Allan Scott
George Scott
George Seaton
Richard Seff
Erich Segal
Paul Selver
Lorenzo Semple
Charles Sellars
Anthony Shaffer
Peter Shaffer
William Shakespeare
Ntozake Shange
Herb Shapiro
Jack Sharkey
Tom Sharkey
Partap Sharma
Anthony Sharp
Dore Shary
Barnett Shaw
Bernard Shaw
Irwin Shaw
Robert Shaw
Toni Sheaver
Marsha Sheiness
Edward Sheldon
David Shellan
Mary Shelley
Sam Shepard
Eric Shepherd
Jack Sher
R Brinsley Sheridan
R C Sherriff
Alan Sherman
Richard Sherman
Robert Sherman
Charles Shertzer
Robert Sherwood
A B Shiffrin
Rae Shirley
Marion Short
Max Shulman
Earl Shuman
Herman Shumlin
Mary Shura
Paul Shyre

39

George Sibbald
Larry Siegal
Gregoria Sierra
Paul Sill
Frederick Silva
Fred Silver
Danny Simon
Neil Simon
Peter Simon
N F Simpson
Campbell Singer
Issac B Singer
Rosemary Anne Sisson
Bernard Slade
Julian Slade
Susan Slade
Frank Slaughter
Charlie Smalls
Betty Smith
David F Smith
Dodie Smith
Michael Smith
Robert Paul Smith
William H Smith
Winchell Smith
Pauline Snapp
Dennis Snee
Michael Snelgrove
Marvin Solley
Bill Solly
Carol Sorgenfrei
Ralph Spence
Ruth Spevis
Bella Spewack
Samuel Spewack
Leonard Spigelgass
Murray Spitzer
Enid Staff
Kathleen Stafford
Lynn Starling
Ben Starr
Austin Steele
Joseph Stein
Cecil Stephen
Rod Sterling
Carl Sternheim
Leslie Stevens
Michael Stevens
Thomas Wood Stevens
Charles Stewart
Anthony Stimac
Brian Stocks
Jacqueline Stoker
Gene Stone
Joel Stone
Merritt Stone
Peter Stoner
Joyce Stoner
Tom Stoppard
Edward Storer
David Storey
Lesley Storm

Alan Strachan
August Strindberg
Austin Strong
Charles Strouse
Aimee Stuart
Preston Sturgis
Jule Styne
Arthur Sullivan
Ruby Sully
Arnold Sundgaard
Dan Sutherland
Evelyn Sutherland
Shaun Sutton
Elizabeth Swados
Francis Swann
Herbert Swayne
Allen Swift
Vernon Sylvaine
J M Synge
Alex Szogyi

T

Richard Taber
George Tabori
Tom Taggart
Booth Tarkington
Ben Tarver
Jules Tasca
A R Taylor
Christopher Taylor
C P Taylor
Don Taylor
Edward Taylor
Ian Taylor
Jeremy James Taylor
Ken Taylor
Renee Taylor
Samuel Taylor
Tom Taylor
John Michael Tebelak
Howard Teichmann
Megan Terry
Peter Terson
Steve Tesich
A C Thomas
Brandon Thomas
Caitlin Thomas
Dylan Thomas
Robert Thomas
Bill Thompson
Jay Thompson
Julian Thompson
Ron Thronson
Lee Thuna
Leonard Thura
James Thurber
Beverly Thurman
Peter Thwaites
George Tibbles
Bill Tidy
Ted Tiller
Byron Tinsley

Fred Tobias
John Tobias
Barbara Euphan Todd
Mel Tolkin
Bud Tomkins
Juliet Tompkins
Gertrude Tomkonogy
Ruth L Tongue
John Peter Toohey
Dan Totheroh
Barbara Toy
Wendy Toye
Jane Trahey
Robert Traver
Ben Travers
Elleston Trevor
William Trevor
Harry Tugend
Joseph Tuotti
Ivan Turgenev
Daniel Frank Turner
David Turner
Oscar Turner
Dorothy Turnock
Mark Twain

U

Peter Udell
Yale Udoff
John Underhill
Franklin Underwood
Rodolfo Usigli
Peter Ustinov
Arnaud D'Usseau

V

Martin Vale
Maurice Valency
Valentine
John Van Antwerp
John van Druten
James Van Heusen
Sutton Vane
Roland Van Zandt
John Varl
Joan Vatsek
Bayard Veiller
Al Ver Schure
Frank Vickery
Steven Vinaver
Allan Vincent
Sean Patrick Vincent
Charles Vites
Paula Vogel
Kurt Vonnegut
David Vos
Frank Vosper

W

Derek Walcott
William Walden
Joseph Walker

Mavis Walker
Ira Wallach
Hugh Walpole
Eugene Walter
Jim Wann
Donald Ward
R H Ward
John Wardle
John Wave
L Ware
Rose Warner
Clay Warwick
James Warwick
Dale Wasserman
John Waterhouse
Keith Waterhouse
Arthur Watkyn
Donald Watson
George Watters
Philip Weathers
John Weaver
Kenneth Webb
Jean Webster
Frank Wedekind
Dunstan Weed
Kurt Weill
Jock Weinstock
George Weiss
Fay Weldon
Colin Welland
Michael Weller
Derek Wellman
Eudora Welty
Orson Welles
Arnold Wesker
Morris West
David Westheimer
John Wexley
Edith Wharton
Mary Wheeler
Peter Whelan
Peter Whitbread
Alfred White
Diz White
George White
Irving White
Jesse Braham White
Theodore White
Paxton Whitehead
Hugh Whitemore
John Whiting
John Whitney
Bert Whittier
Ron Whyte
Sally Wiener
Michael Wild
Hagar Wilde
Oscar Wilde
Percival Wilde
Alec Wilder
Thornton Wilder
Allene Tupper Wilkes

Charles Wilkinson
John Willard
Doris Willens
Alice Williams
E Harcourt Williams
Emlyn Williams
Herschel Williams
Hugh Williams
L E Williams
Marjorie Williams
Nigel Williams
Robert Williams
Tennessee Williams
David Williamson
Calder Willingham
Ted Willis
Arthur Wilmart
David Henry Wilson
Harvey Wilson
Sandy Wilson
David Wiltse
Shimon Wincelberg
Elihu Winer
Christa Winsloe
Jim Wise
Morton Wishengrad
Stanislaw Witkiewicz
Mary Witt
P G Wodehouse
Judd Woldin
Thomas Wolfe
Waynne Wolfe
Ruth Wolff
Kenneth Wollard
Noël Woolf
Cyrus Wood
David Wood
Margaret Wood
Patricia Wood
Aubrey Woods
Edward Wooll
Herman Wouk
Barbara Wright
Richard Wright
Angela Wye
Olwen Wymark

Y

Susan Yankowitz
W B Yeats
Peter Yeldham
Sherman Yellan
Douglas Young
Howard Irving Young
Malcolm Young
Stark Young

Z

Charlotte Zaltsberg
Paul Zindel
E D Zonik
Charles Zwar

PRINTED BY LATIMER TREND & COMPANY LTD, PLYMOUTH

PRINTED IN GREAT BRITAIN